Jewish Family Retreats
A Handbook

VICKY KELMAN

THE MELTON RESEARCH CENTER
FOR JEWISH EDUCATION
THE JEWISH THEOLOGICAL
SEMINARY OF AMERICA

THE SHIRLEY AND ARTHUR
WHIZIN INSTITUTE
FOR JEWISH FAMILY LIFE

THE UNIVERSITY OF JUDAISM

Excerpts adapted from *The Wisdom of the Sands* by Antoine de Saint-Exuprey, copyright 1950 and renewed 1978 by Harcourt Brace Jovanovich, Inc., reprinted by permission of the publisher.

©1992, 1993 by The Melton Research Center
of The Jewish Theological Seminary of America
and The Shirley and Arthur Whizin Institute for Jewish Family Life.
All rights reserved.
No part of this book may be reproduced in any manner
without the written permission of either The Melton
Research Center or The Whizin Institute.

Published by The Melton Research Center
of The Jewish Theological Seminary of America
3080 Broadway, New York, New York 10027
and The Whizin Institute, The University of Judaism
15600 Mullholland Drive
Los Angeles, California 90077

Book design: Jane Brenner

Manufactured in the United States of America

I HAVE BEEN BLESSED along the journey that has led to the completion of this book. For those blessings I would like to thank:

Hanan Alexander, who first encouraged me to reflect on my work in writing; Gail Dorph, Jo Kay, Carol Ingall and Liz Koltun, for thoughtful reading of the manuscript in its many phases; Jane Brenner, Danielle Shelley and Diana Lorentz, who were so helpful in the production phase of the book; Glenn Karonsky, director of Camp Ramah in California in the year the idea was born, who took the risk; the Melton Research Center, led by Barry Holtz and Edy Rauch, which provided the seed money in the initial phase of this project and much faith in me and my ideas over many years; the Agency for Jewish Education of the Federation of the Greater East Bay and the Koret Foundation for the collaboration that initiated Shabbat Camp, the translation of the model to a "neighborhood setting"; Janet Harris for being a wise and energetic partner in the creation of Shabbat Camp; the Whizin Institute, Shelley and Bruce Whizin and Ron Wolfson and the whole "gang" for taking it all seriously; the counselors and staff at both Ramah and Shabbat Camp, who provided the fuel to make it go.

I'D LIKE TO DEDICATE THIS BOOK

    to all the campers—who became my family

    to Stuart, Navah, Ari, Etan and Elana—my family, who became my campers (thanks for the time, the laughter and all those spicebox containers!)

    and to my parents, Charlotte and Sam Koltun, who first introduced me to the joys of both family and camp

Rosh HaShana 5753
Berkeley, California

Contents

1 Introduction 1
  Basic Background and an Introduction to the
    Institutions and Players 2
  Structure of the Book 4
  How to Use the Book 5

2 Why Do a Retreat? 7

3 Zones and Scaffolds: Toward a Theory for Jewish Family Education 9
  Family Education: Why? What?
    For Whom? 14
  Designing the Program for Novices and Experts 16
  How It Comes Together 19

4 An Overview of the Family Retreat/ Camp Setting 25

5 Issues to Consider 27
  Thinking through a Framework for Jewish
    Observance 27
  Choosing a Date 28
  How Long Should a Retreat Be? 30
  Should a Retreat Have a Theme? 30
  Who Is the Target Population for a Retreat? 33
  Marketing and PR 34

6 Practical Arrangements 37
  Choosing a Site 37
    Kitchen/Dining Room 37
    Housing 38
    Indoor Public Spaces 39
    Outdoor Space 39

Support Staff 39
Food 40

7 Program 47
Structure 47
Pacing 48
Content 52
    Text Study 52
    Jewish Family Issues 54
    Music and Singing 58
    Tefilla 60
    Shabbat 66
    Tzedakah 70
Children's Program 71

8 Staffing 77
Role Models 77
Guidelines 81
Staff Training 87
    Before a Forty-Eight-Hour Retreat 87
    Before a Five- or Six-Day Camp 89
    Three Options for Theory/Education Discussion 91

9 Evaluation 93
Collecting Feedback 94
Assessing Data 95

10 Lesson Plans 97
Raise Your Hand If—A Parents' Getting-to-Know-You, Warm-up Activity 97
Paper Bags—A First-Night Program for Parents 98
Individual Incorporations 101
Four-Cornered Nametags 102
Gefilte Fish 104
"Family Stuff" 1: Sentence Stubs 106
"Family Stuff" 2: Paragraphs 108
Family Incorporations 109
Family Banners 110
Family Pizza 111
Drama Games—A Family Evening Program 112
Family Fun Night 114
Singdown—An Evening Program for Families 118
Family Talk Collage 119
Outdoor Adventures for the Family 120
Parent Orientation Meeting 122
Orientation Folder 124

11 Hand-Outs 127

12 Bibliography and Resource List 217
   Family Education 217
      Jewish Materials for Direct Family Programming 217
      Theology, Faith Development and Religious Perspectives on the Family 218
      Important General Literature on the Family 219
   Programmatic Resources 219
      Jewish Resources 219
      Stories 220
      Games 220
      Outdoors/Nature 221
      Crafts 222
      Music 222

13 Glossary 225
   Note on Transliteration 226

1 Introduction

THIS is a book about Jewish family education. Its particular area of concentration is the family camp/family retreat as a setting for the practice of family education. Taking seriously John Dewey's famous adage, "There is nothing as practical as a good theory," we have designed the book to provide both theory (which we hope proves practical) and much practice (which we hope clearly interprets the theory).

This material is drawn from my own professional experience in the rich and intense world of family retreats. I have tried to record what I have learned in such a way that the reader will benefit from a vision of what Jewish family education at a more intense level can be, as well as gain practical assistance, encouragement and inspiration.

It is a book for anyone involved in Jewish family education—rabbi, educational director, teacher, lay person, camp director, JCC staffer, cantor or youth program director. It will probably be of greatest interest to those who want to become involved in family retreats. As a complete handbook for creating a family retreat or family camp, this book is designed to provide guidance from the initial decision to undertake a retreat to the good-bye circle (and even beyond). Those with some experience with camps and retreats will probably find some fresh perspectives along with some new ideas and techniques. As a pick-and-choose resource for other family education settings, this book can provide helpful guidelines on issues such as staffing and program planning as well as full descriptions of programs that can be used (as they are or adapted) in many different settings.

The programs I have been involved with operated out of the Jewish framework of the Conservative movement's *halakhic* (Jewish legal) guidelines. As you read, you will see this orientation reflected in descriptions of certain programs and decisions. Despite this clear perspective, I think you will find that the models described here can be adapted to almost any setting. I have tried to indicate where more traditional or more liberal frames of reference would create other choices.

Basic Background and an Introduction to the Institutions and Players

This book is based on my five years of experience as creator and founding director of Camp Ramah Family Camp at Camp Ramah in Ojai, California, and my two years as director of the Shabbat Camp project of the Agency for Jewish Education of the Federation of the Greater East Bay (Northern California).

The earliest origins of the book go back to the summer of 1986, when I took a nine-week break from my "regular life" and returned to my Jewish educational roots at Camp Ramah (the network of summer camps of the Conservative movement). I had been asked to direct the counselor training program at Camp Ramah. At that time I was becoming more deeply involved in family education. As a staff member of the Melton Research Center for Jewish Education at the Jewish Theological Seminary, I had long been involved in supplementary school curriculum development and consultation. I had just finished creating *Together*,[1] the first family education material published by Melton, and I was involved in persuading educational directors to turn their attention in the direction of the family. I discovered that for many years Ramah had sponsored a series of weekends for families during the winter. However, the staff felt that the weekends needed new energy, and they were looking for a new format and new material. The director, Glenn Karonsky, and I began to explore the possibility of using *Together* as the basis for some of the family weekend programming. At some point early in the process, Glenn asked me to think about a summer family camp. I thought it was an idea with tremendous potential. Before that summer's session ended, we began to explore the feasibility of trying out this idea of a camp for families at the end of the next summer.

I then approached Barry Holtz and Edy Rauch, the codirectors of the Melton Research Center, with the suggestion that we consider some sort of official collaboration between the two institutions. Their enthusiasm for the idea was so great that they agreed that my assignment for Melton for the next year (it eventually turned out to be two years) would be to work with Ramah on creating and directing their family camp. Eleven months later it actually came to pass: twenty-four pioneer families inaugurated the new endeavor. By its fifth year (1991), Family Camp grew to two sessions, and it is ongoing as of this writing.

After two successful summers at Ramah, I was drawn into developing a similar experience for families in my own "backyard," the Berkeley-Oakland area of Northern California. This project, which we named Shabbat Camp, is a program of the Agency for Jewish Education of the Jewish Federation of the Greater East Bay. It

---

[1] Vicky Kelman, *Together: A Child-Parent Kit* (New York: Melton Research Center, Jewish Theological Seminary, 1983-84). A series of nine interactive kits on Jewish themes, which are designed for parents and children to do together at home.

received a seed grant from the Koret Foundation that helped to launch it. Shabbat Camp consists of two weekend family retreats a year. (At the end of the second year we also ran a five-day camp in late June.) The program is entering its fifth year and is an integral part of that community's offerings for families.

The two projects that shape this book are helpful for the similarities they share and the differences between them. Both projects had some outside funding while getting off the ground. The Koret Foundation provided Shabbat Camp with a kind of seed-money grant, which covered mostly planning and advertising (the actual retreats had to break even), and Melton paid part of my salary for the first two years as Ramah Family Camp director.

Ramah was six days long (technically, a half day, four full days and another half day), and Shabbat Camp was less than forty-eight hours long (usually from Friday afternoon to Sunday after lunch). Camp Ramah in California is a spacious site which enabled us to grow to thirty-five families (plus staff and staff families), while our Shabbat Camp site had room for fifteen families at most. Ramah is also a full retreat center site, complete with kosher kitchen, chef, kitchen staff, dining room staff, maintenance staff and use of tablecloths, dishes, sheets and blankets. The site for Shabbat Camp had no staff whatsoever except a caretaker whom we could contact only in case of a dire emergency. (The two of us who were codirectors of the program did all the shopping—food and other—as well as some of the precamp cooking. Counselors swept the dining room.)

Despite these major differences, the two projects sought to create the same kind of experience for families and were guided by the same philosophy. As a result, they were able to provide, each in its own way, a similar strong impact on participants. Shabbat Camp required more condensation and more attention to the kind of details that promote a fast start. It also required making every moment count to a greater degree. For example, overlapping was built into adult study so that Torah study was about family as well as about the Torah text, which made the text more immediately accessible.

I did not find major differences in the populations of the two programs. In general, the Shabbat Camp families were less affiliated and somewhat less Jewishly educated and included more non-Jewish spouses than the Ramah group. Shabbat Camp had mostly hyphenated last names, and Ramah had hardly any. (That says something, although I am not sure what.) Both of the programs included families who were not affiliated with any synagogue as well as families affiliated with Orthodox, Conservative and Reform synagogues. There were single-parent families (usually about one-fifth of the total), blended families, families that included a parent who was not born Jewish and had converted, families with an unconverted non-Jewish parent, families with a parent born abroad (in the Soviet Union, Iran, Israel or South Africa) and families with gay and lesbian parents. The age range ran from newborn through grandparent. Families had children enrolled in Jewish day school, three-day-a-week religious school, Sunday school, Jewish preschool or no Jewish school. Most of the families these programs attracted had children below eight years of age, although Ramah always included a group for campers up to age fourteen (it was always the smallest group). In short, Shabbat Camp and Ramah Family Camp have attracted every kind of family extant today in the American Jewish community.[2]

All these families have felt comfortable and have been able to collaborate to create a community. This is because membership in the family is almost extraneous to the central issues shared by all of them: how to be Jewish and find a way to a meaningful Jewish life.

The differences between these projects have provided experience ranging from the "Cadillac" to the "little red wagon" of retreat sites, from groups as small as 45 to others as large as 250, from retreats as short as forty hours to those lasting six days and from conditions of 120 degrees in the shade to long johns and mittens. Your experiences will probably fall somewhere in these ranges. I hope my descriptions and advice reflect the fact that large groups and small groups, deluxe settings and rustic ones, and all seasons of the year offer rich opportunities for creating community. I have learned from these diverse experiences that Jewish families are seeking what we have to offer. Their hunger to absorb, learn and experience helps make both the two-day and the six-day programs powerful transformative experiences.

Structure of the Book

The book is set up to take the reader from the widest-angle panoramic view of the retreat setting to the most specific details. The first major chapter, "Zones and Scaffolds" (chapter 3), provides that wide view. From there on, we narrow our view continually, trying to track the actual retreat planning process. "Issues to Consider" (chapter 5) contains the broad strokes to guide decision making as an actual retreat begins to take shape. "Practical Arrangements" (chapter 6) for site and food follow next, because it is important to settle these issues before energy is invested in the "Program" (chapter 7), which will be the heart of the retreat. (There is no point in planning the program for a retreat unless site and meal arrangements are firmly set.) As the program takes shape, considerations of "Staffing" (chapter 8) should overlap the programming process. The staff you have available will have an impact on certain program decisions. "Lesson Plans" (chapter 10) and "Hand-outs" (chapter 11) complement and fill out the program-planning process.

The loose-leaf binder format is intended to make the contents more accessible and flexible. It is portable. You can take a copy of

---

[2]The word *family* includes all the kinds of families that exist within the Jewish community at this time. A rough definition fitting the scope of this book is any combination of at least one adult and one child who consider themselves a family.

the menu with you to a meeting with a site director or to a committee meeting. You can easily photocopy the hand-out for the family nature walk or the parents' Sentence Stubs discussion starter. You can add to the binder as you begin to take notes at planning meetings, collect ideas and develop your own hand-outs.

How to Use the Book

There are several primary ways to use this book, but the common denominator is the suggestion that the reader begin with chapter 3, "Zones and Scaffolds." That chapter lays out a theoretical framework for thinking about family education, a framework that guided the work described in the book and provides the key to understanding the details and the relationship of the parts to the whole. If you are not about to run a family camp but are interested in family education, this is also the chapter to read. It will provide you with a way of thinking about the whole field that applies beyond any one particular project.

If you are definitely going to plan a family retreat. Read the book carefully from cover to cover; following this full reading you will be prepared to begin planning your own retreat or lobbying your institution to consider planning a retreat. If you begin the book already charged with the responsibility for planning a retreat, you will want to come back to each chapter when you begin work on your own actual retreat, in order to soak in details as you need them.

For example, reread the section on choosing a site when you are ready to visit sites. Take it out of the binder and take it with you! Use the margins for notes. Take your own site-visit notes on three-hole paper so that you can add them to the binder and keep them. The lesson plans are there so that you can pull the one you need. As you adapt these and collect your own, punch three holes and add them. The hand-outs are there to provide guides or to be used as is. When you create a new one or come across a story or news article you think you might use, three-hole punch it and add it to your collection.

If you have already been involved in family retreats or family education in general. Read the whole book; try to take it in as the record of a particular definition of retreat and the experiments that went along with that definition and can complement and enrich your own experience.

If you are interested in family education in general but are not yet familiar with family retreats. Begin by reading "Zones and Scaffolds" (chapter 3). This is the doorway into a way of thinking about family education that can guide any work you do in this general area. After that, it might make sense to read the section on study (chapter 7), the first part of the section on staffing (chapter 8) and the lesson plans (chapter 10), because they provide a rich resource of programs that are easily adaptable to many settings.

If you would like to lobby your institution to undertake a retreat. Read "Why Do a Retreat?" (chapter 2) and "Zones and Scaffolds" (chapter 3) for the rationale and framework. Skim "Lesson Plans" (chapter 10) and "Hand-outs" (chapter 11) for specific examples and flavor.

If you are involved in the Jewish community in any role, either as a professional or in an avocational capacity. Read "Zones and Scaffolds" (chapter 3). Think about it.

B'Hatzlaha! Good luck!

2 Why Do a Retreat?

Bruno Bettelheim

"We all know that if we wish to concentrate on a very difficult task, we retire to a place where we will not be disturbed by anything extraneous to our undertaking. Nobody doubts that the success of biochemical research requires not only a specific laboratory setting but also a single-minded intentness on what is going on in an often incredibly small segment of external reality. A search into one's own soul demands a parallel absorption in the narrowly circumscribed phenomena of the mind, in a setting which is as carefully designed for its purposes as is the chemical laboratory for its very different type of investigation. Thus any human undertaking which presents serious difficulties demands a special environment and the exclusion of all distracting outside influences."[1]

Shabbat Camp and Ramah Family Camp Evaluations

"Shabbat Camp was an experience of comfort and joy shared by families with the same goals for their children."

"A step outside our busy lives to remind us that there is more than 'surface' daily realities. The richness I experienced in growing up Jewish *can* be there for my children—and more—and for us as a family unit."

"Family Camp was an opportunity to enjoy other families in a beautiful setting, singing, learning new ideas, sharing ideas and past experiences about our own Jewish identities."

"The comfort level was consistently nurturing and yet there was a significant degree of intellectual stimulation throughout. I felt very much a part of the group but didn't sense the formation of any

---

[1] Bruno Bettelheim, *A Home for the Heart* (Chicago: University of Chicago Press, 1974), 205.

'clique.' Everyone was ready to share while maintaining the integrity of the unique characters of their families."

From an Israeli staff member. "I was really skeptical and had this nasty suspicion that people were here only to enjoy a break from kids, cheap vacation, etc. I discovered that every person here was searching for some kind of Jewish involvement in their lives and was willing to work at it given the slightest opportunity, help, validation that it isn't uncool to be spiritual. I was really touched by their desire to do something with so many odds against them. In Israel we have it so easy! *Barukh Ha Shem!* (Thank God!)"

"A time to get away with your family to an unbelievably beautiful place in order to get to know people you might never have met, and should have. A time to share first the intimacy of strangers, and then the wisdom of friends. A time to look at your own life and religious practice from the outside, to learn about stuff you probably thought you'd heard too much about already, and to be astounded to discover that it seems new and useful, maybe for the first time."

"I got a lot more out of coming here than I expected and I'm going home with many things to think about and I'm happy about that."

3 Zones and Scaffolds: Toward a Theory for Jewish Family Education

IN recent years, more and more attention has focused on the potential for engaging the entire family rather than just the child in the Jewish educational enterprise. This book is about one setting in which this approach to Jewish education has taken root—family retreats and family camps.[1] Because *thinking about* educating the Jewish family is a prerequisite for *doing it*, this section of the book introduces a way of thinking about Jewish family education.

Family Education: Why?

Schools[2] cannot "turn kids into Jews." From a traditional Jewish perspective, schools were never intended to produce Jews. Homes were.

In Exodus, chapter 12, in the section which describes the observance of Passover, we read, "You shall observe this as an institution for all time, for you and for your descendants. And when you enter the land which the Lord will give you, as He has promised, you shall observe this rite. And when your children ask you, 'What do you mean by this rite?' you shall say . . ." (Exod. 12:24–26). This is the original form of Jewish education: the family shared an experience that aroused a child's curiosity and led her to ask questions. The answers to these questions constituted the telling of our people's story. At the time of the exodus, the experience-question-answer cycle took place at home,[3] but at some point schools and homes became partners, and the cognitive and skill-based components of answering the child's questions were handled by the school. The

---

[1] In this book, the term *retreat* applies to the forty-eight-hour Friday-to-Sunday format and the term *camp* to the longer, four-, five-, or six-day format.

[2] The word *school* includes all types of schools, from maximal to minimal, unless otherwise specified.

[3] I am grateful to Sheldon Dorph for this analysis, more fully explored in his doctoral dissertation, "A Model for Jewish Education in America," Ph.D. diss., Teachers College, Columbia University, 1976.

school's mission originated in answering the questions that arose naturally from children's personal experiences and observations.

Today we find that the experience-question part of the cycle has also moved over into the jurisdiction of the school. Slowly and in retrospect somewhat unfortunately, this change (evident in the last one hundred years) broke the original experience-question-answer cycle in which home was the locus of Jewish life and schools provided answers to the questions stimulated by experiences. Schools now are expected to provide the entire experience-question-answer cycle.

The Jewish school, like any structure that is forced to bear more weight than it was designed to handle, is in danger of collapse. It needs more support. One of the conclusions of many in the educational community is that the family must shoulder more of the weight. The family must take on (again) a share of the responsibility for providing children with a Jewish life.

Are our families capable of doing this? Not most of them— or, to answer in the famous words of Franz Rosensweig, "not yet." Do most of our families want to learn how? My experience with hundreds of families in several different communities tells me that many of them (more than we are generally aware of) do. Family education is designed to help them reach Jewishly, extend themselves and begin to shoulder some of the responsibility for the "Jewishing" of the next generation.

A Christian educator, Harry Emerson Fosdick, once wrote that religious "education is learning about that which you've already caught."[4] The catching takes place in home and life experience. The learning takes place in school.

People are part of family systems. If we want the children who are our students today to grow up to be Jewish adults, we need to work with the families in which they are living *now*. Bolstering only the child's Jewish identity and Jewish knowledge will have a minimal impact on the family system of which he is a part, and yet our existing educational system is based upon educating the child as if she were an isolated unit.

From a certain perspective, there is really no such thing as an individual. Every individual is in fact a component of a family, and families are systems—complicated systems. We have learned from the field of family therapy that the most efficient way to help a child is to work with the entire family of which the child is a part. In the case of Jewish education, the whole system needs the booster shot of Jewish identity and Jewish knowledge. We must develop programs and contexts within which the family is treated as a system and is the client, in addition to schools where the child is the client.

---

[4]Quoted by Margaret Sawin, *Family Enrichment with Family Clusters* (Valley Forge, Pa.: Judson Press, 1979), 26.

Families themselves are in need of support. We all accept the notion that the family is the primary caregiver/caretaker, but the notion that the family itself is in need of care and nurture is a relatively new notion.

Families live subject to internal flux (divorce, birth, death, remarriage) and subject to potentially overwhelming waves of change from the outside (geographic relocation, the insecurity of the current economy, two working parents, the dearth of adequate daycare, the crisis in our school systems). Many families feel isolated from extended family and from community. Frazzled and overcommitted parents feel the lack of meaningful time with their children.

Even for those children growing up in that "classic" American family (mother and father in their first marriage with their own 2.2 biological children, dog, cat and picket fence), the family is very fragile. Because of children's exposure to the varied experiences of peers who have been through divorce and remarriage and all the concomitant trials and tribulations, family does not offer the security it did in the past. Every child who has heard his parents argue has experienced his own family as being on the brink of shattering. Every parent has experienced the same feeling.

Family education is not designed to return us to that classic nuclear family. It is designed to enhance and enrich the Jewish and family life of every Jewish family, whatever its shape and current membership.

In summary, why family education? *Our schools and synagogues need it.* They are struggling under a burden they were never designed to carry. *Our individual children and parents need it.* They live the greatest and most important part of their lives in their families as part of family systems. The entire system should share in the Jewish experience. *Our families need it.* They are searching for community, for meaningful family time, for a way of being a family that is deeper than what they have found in the current American culture—and they are in need of nurture.

Family Education: What?

What would it mean for Jewish education to take seriously the challenge of creating an educational framework in which the family is the client? It would mean equal emphasis on all three terms: *Jewish, family* and *education*. Jewish—offering substantial Jewish content and authentic Jewish experience; family—providing family experiences as well as a way of thinking about family; and education—supplying a (gentle) push toward movement or change. The key components of such a framework would be *scaffolding* and *empowerment.*

Scaffolding. Think of the characteristics of scaffolding as it is used in constructing a building. It provides support, extends the range of the worker, allows the worker to accomplish a task not possible without its support, enables him to extend his reach and provides safety both physical and psychological. Jewish family education experiences should be designed to support the family as it reaches and extends beyond its current safety range. They should provide the physical and psychological safety to learn something new and try it out without risking a fall.

Scaffolding is a metaphor, originated by Wood, Bruner and Ross[5] as a complement to Lev Vygotsky's theory of the *zone of proximal development*. The zone of proximal development is defined by Vygotsky as "the distance between the actual developmental level (of the learner) as determined by *independent* problem solving and the level of potential development as determined through problem solving *under adult guidance or in collaboration with more capable peers.*"[6] In other words, it is the area into which the learner is ready to move *next*. In terms of looking at how learning occurs, the focus is not on what the learner has *already mastered*, but on what the learner has *the potential to learn* in the future. The scaffold is the support given to the learner as she moves into the zone of proximal development (that is, beyond her independent functioning).[7]

Empowerment. The goal of family education is to empower families to be more Jewish (in any of many possible ways) and to feel more competent to take charge of their own Jewish life as a family.

In terms of Jewish family education, this approach means considering where families are ready and able (with help) to move next. The scaffold provides support as the family moves forward into its Jewish and family zone of proximal development.

An example will help to clarify the concepts of zone of proximal development and scaffolding. Think about how a mother uses nonverbal cues to help her baby learn language. The mother creates the scaffold that enables the baby to give a meaningful response to a verbal offer, which the baby cannot understand yet. For example, the mother makes a verbal offer to the child of an object: "Do you want a banana?" Simultaneously, the mother taps on the table to get the child to pay attention. She picks up the banana and extends it to the child with a gesture indicating that she is offering it. The child's language development is in the zone of proximal development—an area beyond the child but into which the child is ready to move. The gestures and body language provide a scaffold for the spoken words, in that they help the child to learn the words. The scaffold not only helps to successfully accomplish the task (understanding the mother's

---

[5]Discussed in Patricia Greenfield, "A Theory of the Teacher in the Learning Activities of Everyday Life," in *Everyday Cognition*, edited by B. Rogoff and J. Lave (Cambridge: Harvard University Press, 1984), 117–138.

[6]Lev Vygotsky, *Mind in Society: The Development of Higher Psychological Processes* (Cambridge: Harvard University Press, 1978), 85.

[7]Greenfield, "Theory of the Teacher," 118.

verbal communication) but also provides information that, as it becomes internalized, gradually eliminates the learner's need for the scaffold. (Eventually the child will comprehend the spoken language with no need for the accompanying gestures.)[8]

Many adults seem to know instinctively how to scaffold a toddler's transition from crawling to walking. Remove anything potentially dangerous from the child's range. Provide a safe space that invites the toddler to "cruise" using chairs, sofa and coffee table for support. Practice walking holding both of the child's hands. Drop one hand. Stand facing the child, get down to his level and hold hands. Drop one hand. Drop both hands. Move back just beyond arm's length. Step back one step. Smile, encourage, beckon, cheer and so on.

A Jewish learning scaffold contains the same elements: psychologically and physically safe space, invitations to move forward, encouragement and people who care about your progress, can provide the props (scaffolding) you need and will cheer you on.

A family program with the goal of helping the family to become more Jewish should provide scaffolding for the family as it ventures into its Jewish and family zone of proximal development. Designed to provide support, the scaffolding allows the family to accomplish a task beyond its level of independent functioning. Scaffolding extends the range within which a family can function Jewishly. You can provide scaffolding for selected needs. In addition, scaffolding functions like the mother in the above example of early language acquisition: it provides the information, experiences and practice the family needs. A good family education program is structured to provide more scaffolding for more difficult tasks, following a moving zone of proximal development. At the right time, the scaffolding can be removed.

The problem in translating these concepts into the highly complex setting of Jewish family education is that there are no universal zones of proximal development analogous to a baby's first words or first steps. Participants do not arrive with their zones of proximal development typed on their foreheads. The challenge for the educator is to design a program that offers a net of options wide enough to maximize the possibility of catching most people at their zone of proximal development. Success becomes a matter of educated hunches based on experience with programs and people.

As a result, professionals working in this area should be knowledgeable about both Judaism and families. Without this dual expertise it is difficult to identify the zones of proximal development and design the right kinds of scaffolding. Jewish family educators whose area of expertise is the family must acquire more Jewish knowledge. Those with strong Jewish education backgrounds must acquire more knowledge about families.

---

[8]Greenfield, "Theory of the Teacher," 128.

Family Education: For Whom?

While some Jewish families may actively seek out family education opportunities, others who are seeking do not come knocking on our Jewish institutional doors. They do not even know they are looking, or if they do, they are not quite sure what they are looking for. These families are like the fourth child of the Passover *Haggadah:** the one who does not know how to ask. The Haggadah instructs us: You make the first move! These families need us to make the first move, create the program, invite or require participation. Other families may need to be enticed to reach. We need to design a kind of "reaching readiness" program.

One helpful way of thinking about Jewish families is based on a paradigm, currently a center of interest and investigation in the field of education,[9] that describes the differences between expert teachers and novice teachers. This paradigm is a useful way of thinking about the knowledge and skills people bring to interactions and to decision making. Among the applicable findings about teachers is that experts are better able than novices to remember facts, features and patterns in their area of expertise. They are superior to novices in separating relevant information from irrelevant information. Even though the expert knows more and draws from a wider range of experience and information than the novice, she can more rapidly evoke the particular items relevant to the problem at hand.[10]

The concepts *expert* and *novice* offer a way to think about some of the issues raised by the idea of a zone of proximal development. We can visualize each family (and each participant within each family) as standing before a zone of proximal development, like a stream to be forded. The purpose of a good Jewish family education program is to provide the help (scaffolding) the family needs to cross the stream. This, in turn, poses two more questions: What kind of stream is this particular family ready to cross? (What is its zone of proximal development?) and, What kind of help is actually helpful? (What kind of scaffolding meets its needs?)

The expert/novice categories can be applied to participant families for planning purposes. Parenting shares certain attributes with teaching. Every encounter with a child or a situation involves on-the-spot decision making. Both teaching and parenting require attention to more than one thing at a time. In both, we must sort out the relevant from the irrelevant.

As I began to experiment with this theory, I tried to array the families in one of my programs along the expert/novice continuum. I

---

*Hebrew words that appear in the Glossary (p. 225) are marked with an asterisk the first time they appear.

[9] I'm grateful to Gail Dorph for introducing me to this subject and sharing her expertise.

[10] Drawn from David Berliner, "The Development of Expertise in Pedagogy" (paper delivered at the Charles W. Hunt Memorial Lecture at the meeting of the American Association of Colleges for Teacher Education, New Orleans, La., 1988).

began to ask myself, "Novice at what? Expert at what?" I realized that in Jewish family education settings, we actually deal with two continua in which our families may be thought of as expert or novice. We have families that are expert or novice at Judaism, and we have families that are expert or novice at parenting. For purposes of definition:

- *Novice parents* usually are raising their first child or lack a repertoire of parenting skills (regardless of the number of their children).

- *Expert parents* usually are raising at least their second child or their second family and seem to have a repertoire of parenting skills.

- *Novice Jews* are those who are new to Judaism. Some are Jews by choice; some were born Jewish but were raised with minimal Judaism or none at all.

- *Expert Jews* are those who were raised in traditional homes or who have chosen to live a traditional life as adults and have educated themselves Jewishly; in general, they are linked to the established Jewish community.

Because a one-dimensional continuum is insufficient for analyzing this particular population, I have developed the following model for purposes of understanding and planning for our population.

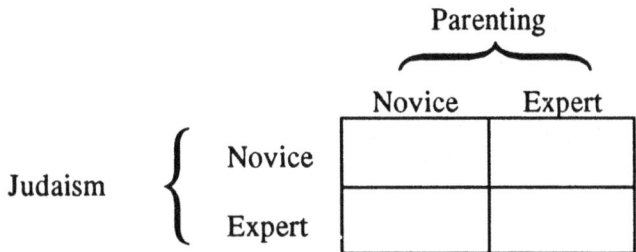

In the planning stages of any family education program, we should insure that programming addresses families in all four quadrants of the chart. If you are dealing with families you know (or, in an outreach program, if you do any kind of intake interview), you may have a good idea which families fit into each quadrant. Sometimes you will do your planning without a clue as to who falls where. However, you can always be sure that you *will* have families in all four quadrants.

This way of looking at Jewish family education—zone of proximal development, scaffolding and the four expert/novice combinations—applies to all kinds of family education programming, from a one-hour classroom experience to a one-week camp. It provides a set of criteria to use in creating and evaluating a program.

Using this set of criteria means that not every program that includes parents and children will measure up as family education. Many programs currently considered family education programs may need to be reclassified or restructured to meet the criteria laid out above. For example, the typical synagogue Friday night family dinner is often carried out in a way that is likely to leave a family feeling even more dependent on the synagogue for its Shabbat experience. The family is likely to conclude that it needs a rabbi and cantor to lead the ceremony, a five-course kosher meal, linen and china and a "cast of thousands." A novice family that draws this conclusion is likely to enjoy the dinner but leave feeling incompetent to have a Shabbat dinner at home.

A Friday evening service or a model *seder** that students "perform" for an audience of parents is no different in kind from a play at school. There is no family interaction component, no learning and moving forward. Each of these old standbys may be a positive and enjoyable experience, but it would not be a Jewish family education experience according to the framework developed in this book.

The Jewish family education model for a Shabbat dinner might involve pairing up two families (one a "Shabbat expert" and one a "Shabbat novice") for a dinner at home or for a large group potluck Shabbat meal eaten on paper plates. Assigned seats help people mix. Tapes and texts provided in advance can be used to help families learn and prepare a "part" they can do together. The Shabbat scaffold for a beginner can be composed of bits as small as information on where to buy Shabbat candles or *hallah** in the community.

Up to this point, I have presented a theoretical framework for thinking about, defining and evaluating the entire territory called Jewish family education. (To the extent that it defines, it also points the way toward evaluation.) This framework holds for all kinds of Jewish family education programs. The remainder of this chapter will concentrate on applying this theory to one specific model of Jewish family education—the family retreat or family camp.

Putting This Framework to Work in Designing the Program

Never assume that everyone knows something. Never assume that no one knows something, and never assume that everyone wants to learn the same thing (or is ready to learn the same thing). Create the experience with lots of scaffolding to make it comfortable and enticing, and complement it with an invitation to learn what is enticing.

For example, create open and inviting discussion starters such as asking people to share a Jewish memory or a memory about something Jewish. Do not base a program on something like a request to "bring a Jewish object from home that has special meaning for your family" unless you are completely certain that every participating family has such an object. If this is the assignment, you will probably lose people before you begin. A safer choice would be to ask people to "bring an object which has special meaning for your family." This is more open and less threatening for everyone, especially those "novice Jews" who may not yet own a Jewish object or who may own one that has not yet acquired special meaning. In response to the second invitation, everyone can bring something; some participants will bring Jewish objects, others will not. Everyone can feel comfortable.

In the same vein and for very similar reasons, a discussion or guided fantasy that takes as its starting point a Jewish memory from childhood can be problematic. Your group is likely to include born Jews without any Jewish childhood memories as well as Jews by choice and non-Jews, none of whom can participate in a discussion based on this premise. You can improve this assignment by making it clear that a person's Jewish childhood may have been a year ago or last week—although this will still exclude non-Jews. (Hence the suggestion at the beginning of the paragraph: share a memory *about* something Jewish.)

Another example of creating an experience with scaffolding is including a range of study offerings in the time slot for *Shabbat** preparation (see p. 166). You might offer a study session on a selection from Abraham Heschel's *The Sabbath*,[11] a reading of a short story or poem about Shabbat, a chance to learn to chant *Kiddush* (the blessing over wine), a "Shabbat 101"[12] for parents of young children, a "Shabbat 101" for parents of preadolescents and adolescents, a Shabbat song session and a chance to make Shabbat table decorations. Such a menu of choices says that the group is varied in terms of background, that you have taken account of this and that it is okay to be a beginner. A person who wants to learn Kiddush will feel validated by the chance to learn a "beginning/baby step" skill, and that validation in and of itself creates a safe environment for learning the skill. The menu also says: There are many ways to welcome Shabbat—find yours.

Program and staff should model clear decision making and unambiguous messages. Learning to set limits is one of the things novice parents struggle with most. One of the ways that a family camp experience can be helpful to these parents is by showing how setting and communicating clear limits helps children and helps the family function more smoothly.

An environment in which limits are a given provides a scaffolding for parents who have difficulty in this area. Parents begin by reiterating the script provided by the setting. "Everyone has to wear shoes outside, that's the camp rule," or "the frogs need to stay in the water." These rules give parents a firm and clear communication, which they are responsible for putting across but which takes them off the hook. They do not have to defend the rule, because it is the

---

[11] Abraham Joshua Heschel, *The Sabbath* (Philadelphia: Jewish Publication Society, 1963).

[12] Shabbat for Beginners, also called "Everything you wanted to know about Shabbat but didn't know where to ask" or "Shabbat with training wheels."

camp's rule, and they avoid the pattern of endless negotiation ("Well, you can take ten steps without shoes"; or "you can pull the legs off one frog"). Another kind of example: "At Shabbat Camp we don't drink milk with meat meals" can scaffold the implementation of Jewish rule setting for the family. Novice parents can learn, from "playacting" with the support of a script, that when limits are clearly stated and unambiguous, something amazing happens—children respond positively to the clarity of the structure.

Unstructured family time is an important component of the program. It offers families a way to practice just being a family. There are families that know what they want to do together when they have free time—fly a kite or find another family to join them for a hike—but there are families who do not have a clue as to what to do with TV-less, mall-less time. Unstructured time is good practice. The resources of the site offer some basic scaffolding in the form of a pool or lake, a ball field, a hiking trail, grass, trees. Other families are also part of the scaffolding. A family unable to mobilize itself may see other families playing frisbee or sitting on the grass playing checkers and then follow suit, learning from their examples. Sometimes it works to offer a loosely structured choice within a free time slot, such as drop-in arts and crafts or a do-it-yourself nature hike (see p. 120). These kinds of activities give the family a framework for practicing being a family.

Across the whole program, the "invitations to cross the stream" should be varied in kind and in degree, taking into account the participants' varying zones of proximal development. This means that one family's zone of proximal development may be to go home with some songs to sing in the car, for another it may be learning *Birkat haMazon* (the blessing after meals) well enough to sing the first paragraph at home every evening, for another it may be meeting another Jewish family that lives in their neighborhood and for another it may be deciding to move a child to a Jewish preschool. The scaffolding happens within the structured program (text study sessions and family issues discussion sessions) and in the informal interactions at the ball field, the dinner table and the pool.

For example, the director of a family retreat recently described her hard work and feelings of failure at being unable to integrate four newly arrived Soviet families with the other twelve families participating in her retreat. Although the Soviet children integrated very well into their age-groups and the families came to *tefilla* (prayer services), the adults did not come to any of the study or discussion sessions and did not mix with the other families at meals. Their written evaluations, however, were very positive, indicating that they had needed to connect with other families in a similar situation to their own (they had not known each other prior to their arrival) and that they had already made plans to get together for Shabbat dinner in two weeks. They did not need to integrate with the American families. The safety of the retreat made it possible for them to find out what they needed, even though their idea of what they needed was not what the retreat director anticipated. The setting she had created enabled them to recognize their own zone of proximal development and provided them with the scaffolding to move across it.

Gather all the information you can that will enable you to more accurately target your planning for all four kinds of families. You can find out about the participating families through an informal phone conversation, which can provide a kind of intake interview. Calling to ask a family, "Do you have any special needs (vegetarian food, access to a refrigerator for insulin and so on)? Do you have any questions or concerns?" often leads to a more wide-ranging conversation that will provide lots of helpful information for your programming.

If time permits, you can survey participants beforehand to find out what they would like to learn or do or participate in during the retreat. (Make no promises except that the input will be taken into account as programming decisions are made.) Asking people what they know can create an uneasy feeling, especially for novices, but people can be tactfully asked what they would be willing to volunteer for (leading the blessings before or after meals, participating in the Torah service, leading aerobics or a nature hike, playing the guitar and so on). Participants can also be sent a check-off list to indicate what they are interested in doing during the retreat. Such a list should include diverse activities: learn to read Hebrew in twelve hours, learn to light Shabbat candles, study some *Talmud*,* folk dance, play basketball, learn origami (Japanese paper folding), discuss toilet training, meet with other parents of pre-Bar/Bat Mitzvah kids, discuss Israeli politics. Some, not all, of this input will help you develop a sense of how your group is arrayed in terms of the expert/novice framework.

How It Comes Together

Working with the definition of Jewish family education and integrating it with the four-quadrant expert/novice schema helps in two ways: in creating programs that meet people where they are and in helping families in many specific ways as the program proceeds. Some stories from actual retreats will clarify and illustrate the theory presented so far.

Novice Parent/Novice Jew

Example. The parent of a two-year-old asks, "I know the three one-sentence blessings that go before Friday night dinner because I learned them from my child's preschool teacher, but I don't know what to do next."

Interpretation. It is not clear exactly what this family is ready to do next. (What is their zone of proximal development?) The facilitator of the discussion makes an assumption that if they have the one-sentence blessings mastered and are learning along with their preschooler, they are ready for five minutes more of Shabbat.

Response. The facilitator suggests "happy times," a Shabbat table tradition she learned in the home of good friends. This activity takes place while everyone is eating hallah and consists of having each person at the table tell a good thing that happened to him during the week that is ending. The parents nod enthusiastically, realizing that this is something they can do, but express surprise that it is "Jewish." They are delighted that they can celebrate Shabbat by incorporating some things they already know how to do. Another parent suggests reading a Jewish storybook as a bedtime story on Friday night. Someone else suggests taking a walk around the block together after dinner. A third person suggests watching a video of "Shalom Sesame" (the Israeli "Sesame Street" series) after dinner. Everyone realizes that they have learned some new Jewish songs during camp that are perfect for singing at the Shabbat table or while taking that walk around the block.

Novice Parent/Expert Jew

Example. A parent is describing the tantrums her six-year-old has been having at the Friday night dinner table. (This is in the context of one of the Sentence Stubs activities, "A Jewish parenting issue I'd like some help with right now is . . . ." See p. 106.)

Interpretation. The facilitator responds by bringing to bear what she knows about the family, an observant couple very familiar with and comfortable with Shabbat observance. The tantrum thrower—the older of their two children—has had three such tantrums during the course of the weekend.

Response. One of the expert parents in the group says, "Tantrums at the Shabbat table are just like tantrums in the supermarket. They're tantrums." This comment helps the novice parent sort out a Jewish issue from a parenting issue. Other parents are able to join in at this point to give helpful hints relating to handling of tantrums. The facilitator who made the observation is also in a position to clarify this further and spend some more time privately with the parent struggling with tantrum problems.

Expert Parent/Novice Jew

Example. In a blended family, a couple with two teenage children and a three-year-old is struggling to explain to their youngest why they do not watch television on Shabbat. The parents have gone into a very complex explanation about the people in the television being asleep on Shabbat, which has only raised more questions and led to more convoluted explanations. They feel that they have become enmeshed in a network of "lies" that is making less and less sense.

Interpretation. This level of observance was not part of family life when the two teenagers were small. Because the Jewish part is so new, the expert parents' knowledge that a three-year-old's "why" does not need the whole scientific/philosophical answer does not transfer to the question about Jewish observance. It had not occurred to them that an answer about something Jewish could be as straightforward as an answer about bedtime or breakfast food. They were novice at parenting a child in a traditional Jewish atmosphere.

Response. Someone suggests that in answer to the three-year-old's "why," they just say, "Because it's Shabbat" or "We don't watch TV on Shabbat." They're amazed at the simplicity of the response but immediately recognize, somewhat sheepishly, that it sounds exactly right.

Example. A single parent explains, "Matt and I have a very nice Shabbat day on the weekends he is with me. Religious school meets on Saturday morning and I go to Torah study while he is in class. We often go out to lunch or go home and have lunch and read together. But *Erev Shabbat** (Friday evening) is impossible for me. Friday is my very worst day at work. I'm exhausted and stressed out, and there is no way that I can get a Shabbat dinner cooked."

Interpretation. As for many novice Jews, it was hard for this mother to separate the information about what is primary to observing Shabbat (in this case, the ceremony that ushers in Shabbat) from information that is of lesser importance (what is served for dinner).

Response. The discussion leader says, "Ellen, bring home a pizza!" Ellen, looking surprised, says, "Pizza? Can you have that for Shabbat dinner?" "Of course. It's the candles and Kiddush and hallah that are the critical parts of the meal. Exactly what is served for dinner is of secondary importance."

Expert Parent/Expert Jew

These parents gain as much from the retreat experience as the others but in a way that is often less obvious. Families who are observant and knowledgeable can feel very isolated in their everyday lives. It is hard to be "the only" Jewish family (or the only Jewish family whose children spend Thursday afternoons at religious school or are expected to spend Friday night at home). These families appreciate most the community celebration of Shabbat and family that the retreat provides. They often respond very positively to the text study opportunities, to the chance to converse with teachers and staff and seek more knowledge. As a family they can enjoy the time to be together, whether it is singing Birkat haMazon or playing frisbee, and they often provide support and encouragement for other, more novice families. One such family (two parents and two children enrolled in day school, traditionally observant Conservative Jews, active in congregational life) wrote in their retreat evaluation, "Thank you so much for the booster shot of Jewishness and of Jewish community. It will energize us for our year's sojourn in the Jewish desert of _____."[13]

In Conclusion

Family education has much to offer all of our families. It meets different needs for each. If we can keep a prototypical family from each quadrant of our expert/novice framework in mind as we plan a retreat, the planning can be less of a shot in the dark and more of a shot on target. If we remember that half of the parents will probably be novices at either Judaism or parenting, we can design programs that provide the scaffolding that makes it safe to cross the stream and also helps them do what novices need most—distinguish the relevant from the less relevant, the primary from the secondary. An effective family education program offers many "fording places" and the unique kind of support needed to ford that stream at that place.

As we design and construct Jewish family education environments for families, we need to ask ourselves four questions:

- *The Jewish question.* What is the authentic Jewish experience embedded in the program?

- *The family question.* Where is the opportunity for the family unit to grow closer, to be nurtured, to gain insight into its own dynamics?

---

[13] A city usually thought of as offering rich and varied resources for Jewish life. Their comment reflects how much they feel themselves to need the family camp experience even though their community offers so much.

- *The education question.* What do we hope families will go home able or ready to do that they were not able or ready to do when they arrived?

- *And the scaffolding question.* Where is the scaffolding, both the invitation to move forward and the support for moving forward?

If we can answer these questions and weave their answers into the work we do, we can affect the Jewish future. In his poem "The Generations," Antoine de St. Exupery says that parents need to take responsibility for their children's education "lest they [the children] allow treasures to rot away because they have not been given the keys."[14] Many of the parents we meet cannot hand the keys to the treasures of Jewish tradition to their children because they themselves were never given the keys or because they have misplaced those keys along the way. In this time and place, it seems our responsibility to give our families the keys to the treasures of their tradition. I have tried to chart one course in that direction.

---

[14] As cited by Roberta Nelson, "Parents as Resident Theologians," *Religious Education* 83, no. 4 (Fall 1988), 492. (The whole poem can be found on p. 185 of this book.)

4 An Overview of the Family Retreat/Camp Setting

A FAMILY camp should create a Jewish context that is fun in the way camp is fun and Jewish in the way our good Jewish summer camps are Jewish. At the same time, it must nurture the family unit. The family camp offers the following elements:

A change of setting. Going to a retreat or camp offers the whole family a new setting, a kind of fresh start. It also offers a situation free from many of the ordinary distractions. There is no telephone, television or computer. There is no need for a car or a supermarket or a mall. This sudden change of space and loss of "props" can be somewhat unnerving, but it can also be liberating. In *A Home for the Heart*, Bruno Bettelheim points out that change of environment is an age-old component of therapeutic experience.[1] The two classic types he singles out are the pilgrimage and the spa. "Pilgrimages seemed to work as a combination of escaping the customary setting and at the [same] time experiencing a more rewarding and stimulating new one . . . leaving the accustomed environment with its demands and routines . . . formulating stimulating new associations . . . concentrating on one's inner voices and feelings . . . ."

Physical togetherness. Families live in one room or one cabin and eat their meals together. This constitutes more together time in several days than most families have in a month (or more).

Balance. Each day is designed to provide a balance of family time, community time and age-group time; of the intellectual, recreational and inspirational; of *Jewish* and *camp*; and of structured time and free time. (For a more concrete view of what this means in terms of a daily schedule, see pp. 145ff. for examples.)

Community. Activities are paced so that people begin to feel connected to one another as they study, play, sing and swim together.

---

[1] This is not to imply that family camp is a kind of therapy. It is therapeutic in the sense of healthy, restoring balance, relieving stress.

As connectedness builds, parents begin to share concerns that they have never spoken aloud before. Their realization that other parents also struggle with many similar issues is validating and strengthening. In the closeness of this kind of communal life, families begin to learn from one another—from observing how other families "do their thing," how they spend leisure time or set limits. Conversations at the pool or at the breakfast table cover issues as diverse as systems for household chores and ways to choose a nursery school.

The outdoors. The proximity to nature is a critical resource for both urban and suburban families. Few families have the chance on a daily basis to sit on the grass and look at the sunset, walk in the woods collecting pine cones, watch gophers burrowing holes, all within a few steps of the front door.

Time for the spirit. People are renewed spiritually by the music, the set time for community prayer, the proximity of the natural world and the atmosphere, which encourages talk about the religious and spiritual dimension of life.

A variety of families. A family camp can include every kind of family on the American Jewish scene today. What do they have in common? With a few exceptions I would say that families (and often staff members as well) share a desire to give their children a more Jewish home and a more positive Jewish childhood than they themselves had. Many of them express the feeling of having missed something valuable that they do not want their own kids to miss out on.

Cross-generational experiences. Family camp community, which can include a range from newborn through grandparent, structures interaction across that spectrum. A six-year-old with no younger siblings will "adopt" someone's baby sibling. A preadolescent will bond with a counselor. A parent may find much to share with a grandparent who is present. A child will adopt a grandparent or a friend's mother. A team for a game or a discussion group will be composed of different ages and sexes and draw upon a variety of talents.

All of these components blend to create a family community that is both spa and pilgrimage and that works to "[renew] the spirit and [give] strength for returning with new vigor to meeting the tasks of living . . . ."[2]

---

[2] Bettelheim, *Home for the Heart*, 202.

5 Issues to Consider

THIS section provides a guide to some of the broader areas that require consideration before actually planning a retreat.

Thinking through a Framework for Jewish Observance

One of the most important preplanning areas is also one of the most delicate: the establishment of a clear halakhic framework for the retreat. If your retreat is under the auspices of a synagogue, the established halakhic practices of the synagogue can serve as a starting place. The congregational rabbi is the person who can help to interpret the synagogue policies as they would apply to a retreat setting. If the retreat is being undertaken by a community agency, it is important to check on what the halakhic guidelines are for community events, although the retreat organizers will probably need some further guidance in terms of how these guidelines might apply to a retreat. If the retreat is being organized by an independent group such as a *havurah* (fellowship group), then the framework should be set by a representative cross-section of participants.

The major retreat areas likely to be affected by halakhic considerations are scheduling and program selection for Shabbat and anything involving food (if any level of *kashrut* (observance of the laws of keeping kosher) is required). Additional areas for halakhic decision making include tefilla (prayer) and *berakhot* (blessings) before and after meals.

The details of planning for Shabbat, tefilla and kashrut are covered elsewhere in this book. You will find help in thinking through Shabbat and kashrut issues in chapters 6 and 7, respectively. Issues concerning food are touched on briefly in the site selection section and taken up in greater detail in the food section in chapter 6.

The halakhic framework will guide your further decision making and help give shape to the environment you are creating. At some point it should be clearly articulated to the participants, so that the social contract is understood by all and the surprises (and embarrassments) are minimized. For examples of how these issues might be communicated, see the precamp letter to participants (pp. 132ff.), the memo to parents (pp. 155-157), and the Shabbat hand-out (pp. 171-173).

Clearly delineated, unapologetic limits also serve another purpose in a family retreat setting. As discussed in chapter 3 (p. 17), such boundary setting can provide a model for parents that demonstrates how clear decision making eases parenting and family life. The parent is assisted to step back from any power struggle with her child because certain things are not her decision. By being able to tell this in a no-nonsense way to a child, the parent may begin to see the positive value in clearly stating a rule which cannot be argued over. This aspect of parenting applies to matters related to halakha as well as to more ordinary components of life.

Choosing a Date

All things being equal, a successful retreat can take place in any season of the year. However, all things are rarely equal, and your actual choice of date will very probably be influenced by two major and overlapping factors: the purpose of the retreat and the availability of the site you want.

Does the Time of Year Make a Difference?

It is likely that the retreat you wish to undertake can take place at any time. However, if you have a specific purpose in mind for your retreat, such as launching a program or helping to build community, you will probably want to hold your retreat at the beginning of the fall. If you want to culminate the year or reinforce community for an ongoing group, you might look more toward the spring or summer.

Does the Season Make a Difference?

In general, a terrific retreat can take place at any season of the year. Each season will yield a different feeling—people may gather indoors around the fireplace or outdoors on the grass—but both work.

However, weather considerations can be very important: Are you in a location where it is likely[1] that weather (snow, for example) could cause cancellation of the retreat or cause people to decide not to drive to the retreat? What facilities does your site offer if it snows, rains or is 120 degrees in the shade? (See the section on choosing a site in chapter 6 for more help in thinking through the interrelationship of site and season.)

Some groups report finding that May is a difficult month to recruit people for a retreat. This seems to be because it is a busy

---

[1] *Likely*, as distinct from possible. Extreme weather is always *possible*, but it cannot really be planned for.

month that includes two holiday weekends already—Mother's Day and Memorial Day, both of which often involve commitments of time and money. This makes it difficult for many families to make yet a third commitment involving a weekend. However, if you choose to plan a Memorial Day weekend retreat, it can give you a longer Sunday and also the potential for an additional day (Monday). Successful retreats have even been held on Mother's Day weekend.

June can be a difficult choice because there are so many weddings, graduations, confirmations and other celebrations. However, in many communities there is a week between school and day camp or regular camp, which can yield time for a weekend or midweek retreat.

Of course, even the above cautions are modified by the size of population from which you are drawing (if you are pulling from a large enough population you can probably end up with sufficient registration although recruitment may be slow), as well as by your track record with retreats and the "tradition factor"—even if you have to struggle to get a Memorial Day or Mother's Day retreat off the ground the first year, next year's becomes "the second annual . . ." and people start to write it on their calendars and their budgets.

The season is also a factor in terms of the Shabbat environment you are creating and the details of your Shabbat programming. When does the sun set? In the winter, can people arrive before dark if this is important? In the summer, can the kids stay up late enough to be part of *Havdalah** if you are waiting for three stars? Obviously this component is shaped by your halakhic framework.

Other Considerations

The Jewish calendar. When are the local Purim carnivals with which families might be involved? Is Federation Super-Sunday a factor? Is there too close proximity to Passover? Is there a major community fundraiser (for example, for the JCC or day school) that might involve the population from which you wish to recruit? Is there a community Israeli Independence Day event with which you do not want to conflict?

The teenage calendar. If you are counting on high school students to be your counselors, note the dates of SATs and PSATs, proms, youth group conventions, finals (and perhaps even major rock concerts).

And do not forget that major American holiday: Superbowl Sunday!

How Long Should a Retreat Be?

The usual format is a forty-eight-hour retreat that lasts from Friday afternoon to Sunday afternoon, conforming to people's orientation to a weekend. However, there are variations on this theme: A three-day weekend offers the chance to add a day; Thanksgiving weekend could give you four days; and winter break, February "ski week" vacation, spring break or summer vacation all yield the possibility of longer spans of time. Consider *Shavuot** (or even Passover!).

A lot will depend on the site—specifically the kitchen arrangements and the living accommodations. If you are doing your own food preparation (see p. 37), more than forty-eight hours can become very trying. Living accommodations that are adequate for two nights may cause everyone to go stir crazy over a longer period of time.

Financial considerations also influence the decisions to be made here. The longer the retreat, the more expensive it will be for participants.

Should a Retreat Have a Theme?

This is a toss-up. It can be helpful to have a theme that ties together aspects of the experience. A theme can also tie your hands. The primary purpose of undertaking a retreat, as articulated in this book, is to provide experiences for the family that are Jewish and fun and that at the same time nurture the family. This is primary. If a theme furthers or complements this, it is a good idea. If it gets in the way of this, a theme is to be avoided.

In general, the more days you have, the easier it will be to work with a theme. You will have enough leeway to organize events that work in with the theme as well as to plan other activities and programs outside the theme. Forty-eight hours may not give you enough time to fully work through a theme and still have breathing space for nontheme activities. Trust your instinct to guide you in making this choice.

A Weekend Retreat with a Theme

A retreat with a Passover theme was held two weeks before the holiday. The Shabbat morning study session was based on Exodus, chapter 12, and an examination of the obligation of the parent (singular) to teach her child the story of the going out from Egypt, along with complementary sections from the Haggadah.

We made the centerpiece song of the retreat "Make Those Waters Part," which is about freedom and various heroes of freedom.

One of the Shabbat afternoon optional activities was to learn (or review) the Four Questions; those who attended received a special commendation at the good-bye circle. The Shabbat afternoon study sessions for parents also included one on "How to Lead Your Own Seder."

One of the Shabbat afternoon study sessions for children over six involved acting out the story of the exodus. On Sunday morning each kids' group made a different kind of *haroset** and we had a haroset tasting before lunch. One kids' group made fancy pillowcases for reclining at the seder.

We had an ongoing display of about twenty-five different Haggadot lent to us by a local bookstore. Parents took time during odd moments of the weekend to look through the collection. They were encouraged to return home to buy the one (or several) they liked and thought they could use.

A Five-Day Camp with a Theme

A Family Camp that took place ten days before Rosh HaShana (and even included *Selihot*[2] on Saturday night) was built on the theme of the New Year as the "Birthday of the World." Adults studied the first three chapters of the creation story in Genesis. This text was selected for its relevance to the "Birthday of the World" aspect of the New Year but also because these chapters lay out some of the basic theology of Judaism—the relationship of human beings to God, human beings to each other and human beings to the earth. This provided an opportunity to enter theology and also begin to do some *Elul*[3] stock-taking.

Because it was the month of Elul, when the *shofar** is blown daily as a reminder to get ready for Rosh HaShana and Yom Kippur, each morning tefilla ended with blowing the shofar. Every child who wanted to had an opportunity to line up and take a turn.

The groups of campers who were six and older studied texts parallel to those the adults were studying. Their text study was complemented by activities such as developing the idea of image by using mirrors; they explored the idea of the uniqueness of each human being by printing designs with fingerprints and by using coins (starting from the *midrash** that compares God and a human king minting coins).[4] Other complementary activities brought them into contact with the wonders of nature (a nature hike whose goal was finding twenty-five shades of green; a study of all the things they could find in a six-inch square of earth; talking about God).

The under-fives made applesauce and decorated jars for honey.

---

[2] The special penitential prayers recited on Saturday night prior to Rosh HaShana, usually at midnight.

[3] *Elul* is the last month of the Jewish year.

[4] Why did God create a single individual first? To show the greatness of God, for a human being stamps many coins from one die and they are all identical, but God has stamped each person from one and yet each human is unique (Mishna Sanhedrin ch. 4:5).

Centerpiece songs dealt with creation: the Hebrew song that counts the days of creation ("VaYehee Erev VaYehee Voker") and "Hinay Tov Me'od."

Each family wrote a letter to themselves with plans and expectations for the coming year. We mailed these to them in time for the New Year. (See p. 177.)

The last evening after Havdalah consisted three parts: a round-robin of preparation for the New Year, with a shofar-blowing lesson, a music session learning the basic High Holiday melody, a sociodrama group in which people acted out a situation that called for *teshuva* (repentance, starting over) and gave advice about doing teshuva, and a table at which families pulled the name of another camp family from a basket and prepared and addressed a surprise New Year card (that we mailed the next week); a chance for families to share the week's text study by creating an interpretation of the New Year through a technique called "Handmade Midrash";[5] and a snack followed by Selihot at 10:00 P.M. (p. 175).

The closing celebration before departure on the next day took the form of a birthday party for the world. Each kids' group worked on preparing a gift for the world in the form of a song. The two through fives sang "Love Is Something If You Give It Away." The next groups sang "Ani V'Ata N'Shaneh et haOlam," "Ya'aseh Shalom," "Yad b'Yad" and Debbie Friedman's "On Wings of Eagles." The counselors brought tears to everyone's eyes with their version of a popular Israeli song, "Yeheyeh Tov," which although taking a somewhat cynical view of world events expresses confidence in friendship and hope in the future. We brought in a huge birthday cake, which had been baked by one group and decorated by another. We actually sang "Happy Birthday" (in English and in Hebrew) and blew out the candles. "Party favors" as people left consisted of a piece of birthday cake and two *Together*[6] kits.

A variation of this in a year with a similar calendar was to hold the Family Talk Collage program (p. 119) before Selihot. The "party favor" that year was a Ziploc™ bag for each family with redwood tree seeds, soil, a small flower pot and planting instructions for "a green and growing year."

---

[5]A technique for interpreting text developed by Dr. Jo Milgrom, which uses just construction paper and glue; see Jo Milgrom, *Handmade Midrash: Workshops in Visual Theology* (Philadelphia: Jewish Publication Society, 1992).

[6]See chapter 1, footnote 1.

Who Is the Target Population for a Retreat?

It is important to design your retreat invitation so that all kinds of families feel included *as families*. Avoid words or pictures that might communicate that you are looking for a specific type of family. Many families are very sensitive, particularly recently reconfigured families. I was once organizing an activity and saw that a mother and ten-year-old daughter currently going through a divorce were sitting in the background. "Come on," I said, "the families have been called in!" The ten-year-old said to me, "Yes, but we are not a family." One congregational retreat planning committee felt so strongly that the word *family* could be problematic that they decided to drop it from their brochure altogether and just call their event the "Congregation Beth El Camp Shabbat."

Every one of the retreats I have been involved in has included all the types of families currently found on the American Jewish scene today. From a quarter to a third of the families at these retreats have been headed by single parents. This mix works. In a retreat setting, families seem to accept each other easily and recognize that, as parents struggling to raise Jewish children, they share the most profound aspects of their lives—more unites than divides them.

A retreat can be either "in-reach" (within a given institution such as a JCC, a synagogue, a synagogue school or a community school) or "outreach" (organized by a central agency for Jewish education or a Federation or other community institution).

In an outreach situation you have an unbounded population to draw from, but on the other hand you have to be careful not to encroach on what other institutions in your community might view as their turf. For example, there might be a community in which the decision by a central agency for Jewish education to organize a retreat would be seen by a congregation or a school as infringing on its area. This does not exclude the possibility of going ahead with such a retreat, but it does mean that you may have to take the additional steps to explain and involve and build partnerships to avoid these pitfalls.

There may also be special subpopulations within your community for which you might decide to tailor a retreat. Although these families easily fit into a large retreat of mixed types of families, they *do* have special needs that require special attention, and they may benefit from the support of other families sharing their circumstances. Such families include single parents, gay/lesbian parents, families with one non-Jewish parent, families that include a member with a chronic illness and families with an adopted child or a special-needs child. Eight or nine families seem to be a minimum number for sufficient social interaction at a retreat (aside from what you might need to break even financially). To attract this many "special families," draw from a large population base, or get a commitment from a preexisting organization or group. In some communities, there may be additional funding available for programming for some of these special families.

Having suggested special subpopulations for whom a retreat might meet unique needs, I must say that in my experience all of our varieties of families benefit when there is a mixture. After the very first Ramah Family Camp, a single parent wrote, "Thank you so much for helping Mike and me feel like just a regular family. Please tell rabbis and school directors that single-parent families just want to be families." In our Shabbat Camp project we organized single-parent Shabbat Camp, which was attended by some families who had been at other Shabbat Camp retreats. Some participants liked being with just other single-parent families, and some participants found the mix of different kinds of families more interesting.

Marketing and PR

In general, your first retreat or camp will require the greatest effort in marketing and recruiting. You have to sell the generic idea first and then the specific commitment to participate.

In an in-reach situation you have a defined target population. Developing the idea with a committee drawn from that population creates ownership of the project and some grassroots support for it. An effective recruiting flyer can be a letter signed by a few of these first committed families that says something like, "We've signed up. Join us!!" Each founding family can recruit a family.

If you are sending out flyers, plan to send three in succession: one to read and lose, one to read and put aside for future consideration and the third one to read and do something about.

In an outreach situation you want to reach the widest possible audience with the news of the retreat. Publicity should include an eye-catching advertisement in your local Jewish paper and in any local publication that reaches the people you want to reach (for example, the family-oriented giveaway found in pediatricians' offices and children's clothing stores or a neighborhood paper of some sort), flyers to go home with every child in every Jewish school (preschool, religious school, Sunday school, day school) and flyers in the places where Jewish parents are likely to pick them up (the bagel place, the exercise place, the kosher butcher).

Brainstorm a list of families known to the planners who may be outside any of the networks mentioned above, and mail flyers with a personal note directly to them.

We have found that it works well to design the flyer using eye-catching graphics but the fewest words possible. A phone number to call for further information is a good recruiting tool if an enthusiastic, knowledgeable person can answer the phone, answer questions, pay close attention to callers' concerns and "sell" the experience. A descriptive piece and applications can be sent out to those who are interested. Once this personal connection has been made, follow-up calls can also be built into the process. (For examples of flyers, application and descriptive letters, see pp. 129ff.)

In an outreach situation, it may help to speak with each rabbi and school director to describe the experience and explain how encouraging families to get involved will in turn enrich their institution. It is often possible to include one of your flyers in a congregational or school mailing or to place a small advertisement in an institutional bulletin or newsletter.

6 Practical Arrangements

Choosing a Site

The choice of a site for the retreat is second in importance only to the decision to have the retreat in the first place. First and foremost, availability of a good site will determine a critical aspect of your retreat: the season of the year. This in turn determines factors such as the type of weather you can expect, candlelighting and Havdalah times and proximity to other holidays (Jewish and American) or community events that might present schedule conflicts. (For more on this, see the section on choosing a date for a retreat, p. 28.) In many communities, desirable retreat sites are booked as much as a year in advance, so you may have to plan far ahead.

Distance and travel time are important factors to consider in choosing a site. In general, the closer the site is to the area you have recruited from, the better. If you want participants to arrive before Shabbat begins, you have to find a retreat site that makes it feasible for them to do so. This involves considering total mileage and traffic patterns in your area. A longer but less congested drive can sometimes be a better choice than a shorter (in mileage) but bumper-to-bumper trip. Some retreats request or require people to take Friday (or at least Friday afternoon) off from work. You might be surprised at the willingness of people to shuffle their schedules once the commitment to the retreat has been made. In general, the longer the retreat, the further participants will be willing to travel.

Kitchen/Dining Room

The first stop[1] in your investigation of a possible retreat site is the kitchen/dining room. Two questions need to be asked before any other aspects of the site become relevant.

1. *Kashrut*. Is kashrut a requirement for your group? If no, skip to question number 2. If yes, which of these setups do you need?

---

[1] This can be done in a preliminary phone call.

____ Vegetarian food cooked in their kitchen would be acceptable; consult on ingredients and menu

____ Kitchen and metal utensils would need to be made kosher; consult on ingredients and menu; supervise cooking process

Get the answers to the above questions first. If kashrut is a given, one of the two above options must be arrangeable. If not, move on to consideration of another site.

2. Who does the cooking?

____ The site provides a cook and kitchen staff

____ It is a do-it-yourself kitchen

____ The site offers a choice between the above

3. Two questions about wine:

____ Does the facility permit wine?

____ Will you need to order kosher wine?

It is always preferable to use a site that takes care of cooking and other kitchen tasks. Running a successful retreat is a very complex undertaking, and if you can hand off the food service, there is one less thing to supervise and worry about—it will make life easier.

For more about the food aspect of the retreat, read the food section (p. 40) very carefully.

Housing

The next critical characteristic of the site to consider is housing.[2] Ideal housing offers each family its own private space (room, cabin or tent) and a private bathroom. In fact, very few retreat centers offer that arrangement, which makes choices more difficult.

Choosing a site at which the family is able to live together is critical to the family component of the retreat. If the kids are living in another building or room with their counselors, the retreat tends to become either an adult weekend with separate childcare and some family time or two parallel programs that cross paths at specified points.

See how close to the ideal you can come. Often you will find something like a lodge, with private rooms and shared bathrooms, or small separate cabins sharing a central bathroom. Sometimes a cabin built for nine or fifteen summer campers can be used by a single family at a retreat.

You may come across sites that offer a mixture of kinds of housing. Such a site is not a problem as long as you can give people

---

[2] You can get some of this information in a preliminary phone call, but you really need to *see* the housing (along with all the other facilities) before committing to the site.

a choice: provide a brief description of housing type, priced differentially if differences in housing are substantial, and assign housing according to choice on a first-come-first-served basis.

Other questions to ask. Do cabins/rooms have electricity? Is there heat? If not (and if this could pose a problem), is electric wiring sufficient to permit people to bring portable heaters? Is there air conditioning? Can people bring fans? Consider the distance and any considerable uphill or downhill grade from the cabins to the dining room and main meeting places. Can toddlers walk it? Is it possible to push a stroller? A wheelchair? Can an older person walk it?

Study the housing with an eye to how you would organize the *shmirah* (babysitting system) during the adult evening program.

Indoor Public Spaces

What other indoor public spaces does the site offer? What kinds of spaces are there for whole-group gatherings? Is there space which can be set aside for tefilla? For adult study sessions? For evening programs? Is there sufficient indoor space if the weather is bad?

What kind of seating is there—chairs? Benches? The floor? Will chairs have to be carried from place to place for different programs? (If so, will participants need to do the carrying or is there a site staff that can do this?)

What is the distance from these spaces to the sleeping quarters and the dining room? Will the time it takes to get from place to place be a consideration in programming?

How far are these gathering spaces from public or cabin bathrooms?

Outdoor Space

What kind of outdoor space is there? First, if there is a pool and it is not gated and locked, this site is not acceptable. If there is a lake or pond, how much of a hazard might this be for your group?

Are there playing fields and courts, hiking trails and climbing equipment? Is there an outside amphitheater that could be used for tefilla, singing or a talent show in nice weather?

Support Staff

What kind of support staff will be on site during your retreat? What is the procedure if something malfunctions (a toilet overflows or there is no hot water or toilet paper)? Is there someone who sweeps the dining room? Cleans the public bathrooms?

Miscellaneous Thoughts on Sites

In general, hotels are not good retreat sites. There are too many distractions. Sometimes universities (particularly during the summer) will offer something closer to the ideal.

You may end up choosing a site that necessitates kids sleeping in cabins by age-groups, with adults sleeping separately (perhaps parents with private rooms or women and men dormitory style). This choice definitely lessens family togetherness during the retreat. However, if no other viable option is available, you might go with this setting and build more family time into the daytime program to balance the housing factor.

Can families use their own tents or campers? Most places have a policy covering this. Keep in mind bathroom and shower use for tents and campers.

Food

Good food, and lots of it, is critical to the success of almost any gathering we can think of—all the more so when people are away from home and far from their usual (and comforting) sources of food. This is not to say that the food must be fancy (people who are coming to camp know they are coming to *camp*), but it must meet those two criteria of good and plentiful.

Some considerations bearing on kashrut and cooking were discussed in the last section. Keep in mind that it is always easier to have someone else do the cooking. That is why there are restaurants and takeout food! In addition, you will probably find that the prices charged for meals at a retreat site are very competitive with what you can do, even if you do your own cooking. This is because such places tend to order and stock food and other supplies in huge quantities and because part of their expertise as a retreat center is knowing the right kinds and quantities of food.

Is Kashrut a Factor?

There are two basic ways to go if kashrut is a factor:[3]

1. Make the kitchen kosher (oven and burners and all metal pots and implements) and bring in a cook who can prepare all your food on-site. (This is the most complex alternative.) Basins, sponges and towels for washing the utensils must also be brought along. You will need disposable plates, bowls, cups and eating utensils.

2. Make the oven kosher.[4] Have your main course for each meal prepared in the city and brought in large foil pans to be heated in

---

[3] This is neither a comprehensive guide nor a halakhic statement, only a guideline. Consult a rabbi for help with the decision-making process.

[4] If the site you are renting cleans the oven thoroughly after the group that has preceded you, this may only involve running the oven and the burners on high.

the oven, and have the rest of your meals consist of cold food. (See the menu on p. 43.) Hot water for hot drinks can be kept ready in large hot water/coffee pots.[5] Utensils for serving, mixing and preparing food will need to be brought from the synagogue or school, bought new or borrowed from someone who has a kosher home. Basins, sponges and towels for washing the utensils must be brought along. All food is eaten on paper plates with disposable plastic utensils.

Kitchen and Dining Room Staff Considerations

For the first alternative above, you will need a cook and a kitchen organizer who will see to it that setup for the next meal and cleanup afterward go smoothly. This person works with the cook but is mainly responsible for supervising the administration of the meal service and dining room.

For the second alternative, you will need two kitchen staff people. As you will not have a cook, you will need someone with kitchen know-how and administrative sense who can work fast and under pressure. This person can be a competent high school senior, a college student or an adult. The second person (kitchen assistant) can be a responsible high school student.

In both cases, depending upon the size of your group and the facilities, you may need to create a rotation of counselors to help with setup and cleanup. Another option is to give families a share in the running of the dining room by assigning each family a specific meal and responsibility. (The feasibility of this approach will of course vary according to the composition of the families in your group.) It may also be possible to offer a parent or two who is in need of financial aid an opportunity to take on some responsibility in this area in exchange for a discount on the retreat fee. Having the oldest group of children take responsibility for setting up a meal (lunch is often best) under the guidance of their counselors also works quite nicely.

Hints for a Smoothly Running Dining Room

- Serve all meals buffet style.

- Set tables with paper tablecloths or placemats. Put salt and pepper, pitchers of water, cups and silverware on the tables (the latter items can be stacked; places need not be set).

- For meals that begin with saying the *haMotzi** blessing together, it is helpful to have the bread on the tables as people come in so that they find seating first, say the haMotzi together and then come up for the buffet.

---

[5]In most kashrut systems, these will not need to be kashered as they have held only coffee or hot water.

- The fastest, smoothest traffic flow is the most desirable. For this reason the ideal setup would be a long buffet table with plates and identical food laid out from the two ends toward the middle. People can take a plate and move down either side of the table toward the middle. This yields four lanes.

- The one hitch to the buffet style of serving is that younger children do not always have an accurate idea of the appropriate quantity or variety of food to serve themselves. You can avoid this common pitfall by having children come through the line with a grown-up or having staff members helping to serve some of the foods such as chicken and kugel that are trickier to handle.

- Every meal setup should also include peanut butter, jelly and sliced bread (for those with more discriminating palates).

Sample Menu for a Forty-Eight-Hour Weekend Retreat

This tried-and-true menu was developed for arrangement number two above but is a good one regardless of the kitchen arrangement.

Erev Shabbat
    Hallah
    Wine/grape juice
    Chicken**
    Pasta salad**
    Green salad tossed with dressing
    Brownies and fruit

Shabbat Breakfast
    Granola and Cheerios
    Milk and yogurt
    Hard-boiled eggs**
    Orange juice
    Grapefruit sections
    Bagels and cream cheese

Shabbat Lunch
    Kugel**
    Tuna Salad
    Salad bar: lettuce, carrot sticks, cucumber slices, red or green pepper strips, olives, sunflower seeds, broccoli flowerets, garbanzo beans
    Sliced bread, peanut butter and jelly
    Various salad dressings
    Orange sections and cookies

**Double asterisks indicate items brought to the retreat site already cooked.

Se'udah Shlishit*[6]
    Taco shells, flour tortillas
    Refried beans**
    Rice**
    Shredded cheese
    Shredded lettuce
    Chopped tomatoes
    Salsa
    Sour cream
    Sliced bread, peanut butter and jelly
    Ice Cream

Sunday Breakfast
    Muffins or bagels
    Cream cheese
    Granola and Cheerios
    Yogurt
    Hard-boiled eggs
    Orange juice

Sunday Lunch
    Sandwich bar: sliced bread, tuna salad, peanut butter and jelly, egg salad (if there are leftover hard-boiled eggs)
    Chips and salsa
    Any and all leftovers (except meat)
    Fruit
    Cookies

---

[6]This is clearly the point at which to mention regional differences in American Jewish cuisine. Obviously this particular menu represents the California influence. Your population might prefer the traditional herring or go for lasagna, blintzes or grits.

Snacks for a Forty-Eight-Hour Weekend Retreat

Arrival
    Peanut butter and crackers
    Apple juice

Late Erev Shabbat (for Adults and Counselors)
    Pretzels
    Mixed nuts
    Fruit
    Wine
    Juice

Shabbat Kiddush (after Morning Services)
    Kids: grape juice, cake slices
    Adults: wine, grape juice, cake slices

Shabbat Afternoon (Approx. 4:00 P.M.)
    Kids: apple juice in boxes, granola bars (counselors take with them to groups)
    Adults: fruit, trail mix

Saturday Night (for Adults and Counselors)
    Cheese and crackers
    Fruit
    Chips and salsa
    Wine
    Juice

Menu for a Five-Day Camp

This menu was developed for a retreat where we did our cooking.

Wednesday
- Lunch: sandwiches (tuna, egg salad, peanut butter and jelly), chips, salsa, nectarines and peaches
- Dinner: Spaghetti, meat sauce (tomato sauce for vegetarians), bread sticks, green salad and dressing, fruit

Thursday
- Breakfast: bagels, cream cheese, granola, yogurt, Cheerios, orange juice, milk, coffee
- Lunch: baked potatoes and toppings (grated cheese, olives, butter, sour cream), green salad and dressing, fruit
- Dinner: pasta casserole, green salad, garlic bread, cookies (baked by kids in afternoon)

Friday
- Breakfast: same as Thursday's except muffins instead of bagels; also, hard-boiled eggs and mayonnaise
- Lunch: quesadilla, salad bar, fruit
- Dinner: Hallah (baked by participants), rice, green salad and dressing, chicken, brownies (baked by kids), fruit

Shabbat
- Breakfast: the same
- Lunch: kugel, fruits served salad-bar style, yogurt, cottage cheese, raisins, egg salad, hallah (from a bakery)
- Se'udah Shlishit:* taco bar (tortillas, rice, refried beans, grated cheese, olives, salsa, sour cream, lettuce), ice cream and chocolate syrup

Sunday
- Breakfast: the same
- Lunch: sandwich picnic

7 Program

Structure

One of the best-loved Ramah Family Camp evening programs is Family Fun Night (p. 114), and one of the favorite activities within that program is the game Blockhead, in which players take turns placing odd-shaped blocks to build a tower that is as high, yet as sturdy, as possible. The building of a retreat is a lot like the building of the Blockhead tower. A carefully selected variety of small blocks go into the construction of a sturdy retreat. They are put together with care for balance, fit and aesthetics.

By Age-Group

There are blocks of time that are organized by age-group. Adults have study time, discussion time and free time for recreation (swimming, tennis, basketball, aerobics) or just doing nothing. Kids, organized into age-groups in a way that makes sense for the population of a given retreat, enjoy counselor-organized activities including study, swimming, new games, crafts, outdoor/nature activities, singing, dancing and drama.

By Family

Other blocks of time are devoted to family time. Some of these are completely unstructured, with no camp facilities and no staff available. Families can choose to fly a kite or take a hike, toss a frisbee or read a book together, sit on the grass and shmooze or play checkers with the family in the cabin next door. Some of these blocks make camp facilities available for families to choose activities such as swimming or kickball. Some provide a choice of optional structured activities such as open arts and crafts (offering one or two projects for collaboration) or a chance to play *Hide and Seek: A Game About God*,[1] learn some origami or join a nature adventure (p. 120).

---

[1] Kit #5 in the *Together* series; see chapter 1, footnote 1.

For the Whole Community

There are blocks of time that involve the whole community as a community. Tefilla is one of the prime community times. This includes morning tefilla, Shabbat tefilla, the Birkat haMazon blessing after meals and Havdalah at the conclusion of Shabbat. Everyone is doing the same thing at the same time, and the experience itself is enhanced by the community's presence. Singing and dancing are both powerful community-building times. There are other community times during which each family is working as a family unit and all the families are involved in a parallel activity. Hallah baking is this kind of activity. The flour is flying; music and the smell of dough fill the air as each family works on its own hallah in close proximity to all the other families making their own. Many evening programs have this characteristic—for example, each family making its own banner to share (p. 110) or preparing its own skit to present.

Pacing

The pacing of the entire retreat requires careful attention. Within the retreat itself, beginnings and endings require the most meticulous attention to detail. Families need help in making the transition to camp and community, and they need help in taking stock of the experience, saying good-bye and heading for home.

Getting Going/Warming Up

The first major task of the retreat organizers is to orient people to the physical site, answer their most immediate questions and concerns and help people get to know one another.

Open the retreat with care. Meet people as they drive in. Direct them to cabins and parking. If you have enough staff, make them available to assist families with the unloading and shlepping of their gear. Have orientation folders prepared. (See p. 124 for a list of what might be in the orientation folder.) Serve a snack if people have been on the road a while and it will be some time before lunch or dinner.

Provide people with nametags. We actually put preprinted nametags for each adult in the orientation folder, along with the children's nametags, which are usually made by their counselors and which include the child's name and a symbol of some sort to identify the child's group. If you use the peel-off-backing type, provide each person with three tags: one for right away, one for Shabbat (which avoids a possible halakhic problem of writing on Shabbat) and one for Sunday.

Assigned seating for the first two meals (excluding breakfast, which tends to be more buffet and less scheduled) is a must. Mix new and returning families. Match families by age of children or by common interest (if you know it) or arbitrarily by sizes of families that fit around whatever size table you are using. This goes a long way toward alleviating the anxieties that everyone shares when entering a room full of new faces. It also communicates the care with which the experience has been put together. Figure out the seating chart on paper, and then make assignment cards for each family like the ones used for wedding and banquet seating. (Use three- by five-inch cards folded in half. Decorate with a sticker.) Set them out in alphabetical order near the dining room door. Remember to put a number sign on each table, too!

The first four hours of a weekend retreat. If people are arriving just prior to Shabbat and your halakhic framework requires that you get going with Shabbat at sunset, provide the most important parent information in a written memo in the orientation packet (pp. 155ff.). You can try to gather everyone for a five-minute meeting before candlelighting so that you can give them the most important information and tell them that there will be time later for a parents' meeting. If most of the participants do not know each other, getting Shabbat going can feel a little stilted. Shabbat is ideally a celebration of community, and people who have just met cannot be a community. Whether *Kabbalat Shabbat** precedes or follows dinner will not be the major factor here. If the getting-to-know-you portion of the evening really has to follow both, it will just take time.

A model that weaves together Oneg Shabbat* and getting-to-know-you. Follow Birkat haMazon with a song that can be sung as the leader or song leader dances people away from the tables and leads them into a circle dance. Ask people to hold hands or link arms with members of their own family. Direct a game of Incorporations[2] (p. 109) composed of about four to six rounds and winding up with Ring-around-a-Rosy. Families can then easily merge into one large circle again for two quickly learned (thirty seconds each) dances: *mayim** and *cherkassiya.**

Cherkassiya, a dance in which a different person leads each section of the dance (choosing a step or action or mime movement of his own), can lead easily into dividing children by age-group[3] so that the children end up in circles with their own counselors and then have a short group activity. This step is critical because it lays the groundwork for the next morning when children will go off with the counselors after tefilla. It provides children with a sense of familiarity with their counselors and other group members, which should facilitate the next morning's separation.

The groups can spread out away from each other and take fifteen to twenty minutes for getting-to-know-you games and circle

---

[2]Incorporations is the ideal mixer game for this kind of evening because it uses no supplies, requires no reading or writing that might exclude younger family members and fits any halakhic setting.

[3]We usually make this easy by coordinating the kids' nametags so that a color, symbol or sticker designates each group.

games. The parents can be pulled aside and the time used to explain how the evening shmirah system will work, so that they will feel comfortable leaving their kids and returning for the adult evening program. I like to use the rest of the time for an informal game of Raise Your Hand If . . . (p. 97). After about twenty minutes, gather the whole group together for some quiet Shabbat songs (ones you think are in the "public domain" such as "Shabbat Shalom," "Mah Yafeh HaYom," "Oseh Shalom"), a lead-and-follow song and then your good-night circle.

When parents return later for their evening program, hold a short, fifteen-minute meeting in which you review what was contained in the parents' memo in their packet, stressing what you think is critical and answering any questions. The evening program should consist of a mixer that gets people talking and feeling comfortable with one another and also raises (in a minor way) some of the weekend's topics. Suggested programs include Paper Bags (p. 98) and Individual Incorporations (p. 101).

The first four hours of a family camp that begins midday on a weekday. Gather everyone for some celebratory singing. Introduce the few people whom everyone needs to recognize right away (the director, the doctor, the head of the pool). Have kids stand up in groups by age (starting with the oldest group) and walk to one side or outside with their counselors. While they spend fifteen to twenty minutes in getting-to-know-you games and circle games, the parents can be drawn into a game of Raise Your Hand If . . . . Everyone can reassemble for two or three songs before heading to change for swimming. Later in the afternoon, children will go off for group time with counselors and kids they have already met. Parents can gather for a short meeting covering the essentials and then begin their studies.

The family evening program (following dinner with assigned seats) consists of a game of Incorporations followed by a collaborative family project such as Family Banners (p. 110) or Family Pizza (p. 111) and good-night circle.

The parents' evening program can be the same kind described above for Erev Shabbat.

Keeping It Going

Building community does not stop with the first evening, no matter how successful it has been. Ten families may actually feel like a community after the first day, but thirty probably will not. The community-building factor will also be influenced by how many people know one another before coming to camp. It is important that people continue to wear nametags. With groups of about twenty families, we often have used a mealtime quiz whose goal is to get people introduced and talking. It might be a riddle ("Where is baseball mentioned in the Bible?"), facts about the site ("What do you think the temperature will be today at its highest?") or information about the families present ("Which family traveled the most miles to get here?" or "How many Sarahs do we have in camp?"). For examples, see p. 167.

Whether the next portion of time you have is a day and a half or a week, balance and variety are the secrets of success. The schedule should reflect the principles of balance outlined above. It is also important to avoid overprogramming. This is a particular pitfall within a weekend retreat because the time seems so short and the temptation to pack everything in is so great. A critical part of a successful retreat experience is time to take a walk in the woods or sit and contemplate the trees. The schedule has to respect the need of the participants to assimilate and absorb their experience. Neglecting this can lead to overload and shutdown. The schedule also has to provide time for participants to share their reactions and experiences and life stories with one another on an informal basis. Many of the most important connections between people come about in this way.

Wrapping It Up

As much care should be given to closure of this intense experience as to getting started. In all settings, wrapping up should involve making available to participants copies of all study materials, tefilla and song sheets and Birkat haMazon sheets or cards to take home with them. (These provide a kind of portable scaffold to support them at home.) It also should include lists of phone numbers and addresses of all participants and staff members. (This is another component of the scaffold, which maximizes the possibility that participants will maintain their friendships.) Ideally, wrapping up would include an invitation to a "reunion"[4] to be held at a specific date and place, far enough in advance so that chances are good that people can save the date. (This is a third kind of scaffold.)

The closing celebration might include a family camp "museum" displaying crafts that children and families have executed during the retreat. Depending on the size of your group (and the weather), it can be a circle in a pretty outdoor spot or a gathering indoors. It might feature a special edible treat prepared by the children. It might include a presentation—by kids or adults or specific families—of a song, dance or skit. Music is a critical connection and community builder. Reprise all the special songs that people seemed to find moving and expressive, and end with the one you feel works best to connect people and capture the kernel of the camp experience. (See page 32 for a description of one closing celebration.) This is the time and place for the culmination of a *tzedakah** project if you have undertaken one (see p. 70).

At Ramah Family Camp we always included a family camp song in our closing celebration. Doing this involves choosing an easily singable song (such as "Row Row Row Your Boat" or "This

---

[4] Successful reunions have included a Sunday afternoon picnic, a potluck Erev Shabbat dinner at someone's home, an outing to the ballgame and a seder.

Land Is Your Land") and writing a chorus for all to sing, which expresses something about Family Camp (p. 195). In advance of the closing program, everyone is taught the chorus (after a meal or similar gathering time), and families are invited to write their own verses. At the closing celebration, each family has a chance to sing its own verse, with everyone singing the chorus between the verses. An activity like this gives each family a collaborative project involving composition (which is a way of providing scaffolding for a kind of stocktaking of the experience), rehearsal and presentation (a moment of family pride). At the same time, it provides a group review of the experience, which is also an expression of community.

Content

Everyone at a retreat is learning all the time, but there is a need to establish set times for more formal study. Parents coming to a family retreat are in need of two kinds of study. They need to add to their own Jewish knowledge, and they need the opportunity to confront and share with other parents their ongoing struggles to be a Jewish family in this culture in these times. Even a forty-eight-hour retreat, during which there might only be time to squeeze in three hour-and-a-half sessions, can be designed to include time devoted to study.

Text Study

At the first Ramah Family Camp, we decided to make traditional text study the key community experience for the adults. We felt that challenging adult text study could serve as the core of a successful retreat. Our intuition was that many parents, even those who are attracted to the relatively intense Jewish experience offered by a retreat, view Judaism as something "for the children." They may choose the retreat for the children or for the family without knowing that there is something in it for their own personal growth as well. Many have not studied anything Jewish since their own childhoods (if then), and many may not have studied anything (aside from professional in-service courses) since their entry into the work force.

It seemed to us then (and our experience has more than borne this out) that a retreat is the ideal time to offer serious, intellectually challenging and exciting Jewish text study. The choice of text study experience (over how-to skill sessions) is also anchored in a firm preference for the experiential model rather than the skills model as a mode of structuring the retreat experience. Whereas a skill-learning session usually functions to separate those who do not "know how" from those who do "know how," a carefully selected text in the hands of a skilled teacher can always be peeled back to reveal yet another layer of meaning even to a person who has already studied the same text. It is important that the mode of study require students to be active inquirers *into* the text as opposed to passive listeners to a lecture *about* a text. Shared text study can be a major force in creating community out of a group of relative strangers. The study session provides a setting in which people can get to know one another as they share ideas, reactions and personal revelations in a safe and fairly structured environment. It also provides some of the issues and questions and ideas for conversations at dinner or at the pool throughout the rest of the retreat.

Over the five years of Ramah Family Camp, we have found that the morning adult study session has proved to be a favorite time of the day for participants and a focal point for sharing the ideas, insights, thoughts, and laughter that characterize a community.

In a Four- or Five-Day Setting

Our choice of text for the first year was the cycle of Joseph stories. We made this selection because we felt it provided an opportunity for an exciting narrative text that was also about family, making family both "text" and "subtext" in class. The discussion was about Joseph and his family and the roots of the Jewish people, but it was also about the families represented in class—experiences with mothers and fathers and siblings and with being a mother, a father, a parent of siblings. One year (during which camp took place the week before Rosh HaShana), we studied the first three chapters of Genesis. (This selection reflected a desire to connect study with issues raised by the High Holy Days: our relationships to God, other people and the earth.) Another year, we looked at different prayers as ways of defining and understanding God. More recently, we studied *U'N'Taneh Tokef* (the central prayer of the Rosh HaShana/Yom Kippur season), exploring the metaphor of being "written in the book" and confronting the finiteness of life and its unpredictability. We also studied the Torah readings for the two days of Rosh HaShana—the Hagar-Ishmael story and the story of the binding of Isaac, focusing on Abraham as the parent, certainly his most problematic aspect.

In the five-day retreat that I directed for the Agency for Jewish Education in June 1990, the adult text study was the Jacob-Esau stories. We selected this text for reasons similar to those for selecting the Joseph cycle for the first Ramah Family Camp.

During a five-day or six-day retreat, text study can be a daily experience, and there will still be other time available for discussion of Jewish family issues.

For a Weekend Retreat

Total adult study/discussion time at a weekend retreat is probably limited to two or three sessions, so time for pure text study is even more at a premium. We have found a way to condense and blend text study with discussion centered on family issues (see p. 55).

Jewish Family Issues

It has been our experience that one of the things needed by parents who come to a family retreat or family camp is the opportunity to explore issues related to the struggle to be a Jewish family in America today. Participants do not necessarily articulate this need a priori. That is, parents themselves may be only dimly aware of this as a need. However, it can be clearly discerned in the way they respond to the opportunity to discuss topics in this general category. Over the five years that I have spent running family retreats and family camps, I have *never* opened up this subject to a less than enthusiastic response. I always have the feeling that the questions and quandaries and doubts and worries that parents experience in this area are just below the surface, almost waiting for the chance to jump out on the table for discussion, sharing and reassurance.

Several necessary components for these discussions include the invitation to talk about these Jewish family issues, an open non-judgmental discussion structure that provides safety for the sharers, a structure that fosters support from participant to participant and a guiding hand from the experience of the facilitator.

What emerges first of all from this type of study/discussion (when it works) is that participants feel relieved and heartened to discover that almost everyone struggles with similar issues. They receive some help in the form of general insight and some help in the form of specific practical suggestions (from other participants or from the facilitator). They are encouraged and supported in the loneliness of the struggle. And the sense of community within the group is heightened by the kind of sharing that happens at this level.

The exploration of what it means to be a Jewish parent and to create a Jewish family is what provides meaning to everything else that happens during a retreat, whether it is studying a text, learning a song, making a spicebox or playing frisbee. This exploration is what provides the context into which everything else fits.

In a Four- or Five-Day Setting

- *First-night parents' evening program.* Begin to raise some of the issues in the getting-to-know-you activity. These can be part of the fun of the icebreaker games, giving lighthearted and nonthreatening peeks at the issues—but at the same time also conveying a sense of framework and expectation for the retreat as a whole. (See the pacing section of this chapter, p. 48, for more on this, and turn to pp. 98ff. for several specific examples of evening programs designed to accomplish this goal.)

- *A chance to talk about "family stuff" at an evening program:* We always devote at least one additional evening program to "family stuff." The three formats that work best for an evening program (complemented by snack and Israeli dancing or informal group singing) are Sentence Stubs, Paragraphs and *Gefilte Fish*. In Sentence Stubs, each participant writes out, during some quiet time, the ends to a series of sentence beginnings. Following this, people form groups of six to eight (preferably with spouses joining different groups), and each person has a few minutes to share one of her sentence completions (p. 106). In Paragraphs, participants receive a two-page hand-out with ten paragraphs about different aspects of family life. People are asked to form groups of people interested in discussing the same paragraph (p. 108). *Gefilte Fish* is a fifteen-minute videotape featuring interviews with three generations of women from the same family about their divergent approaches to making gefilte fish. It is very humorous, touching and insightful in terms of generations and traditions (p. 104).

- *Other formats.* Optional family-talk sessions can be offered during some of the time slots when children are in groups with their counselors and parents have free time. These sessions will attract people who prefer to take advantage of the chance to discuss family issues with other parents, guided by a skilled facilitator, rather than play tennis. Depending on the topic, such a session is also an opportunity to address the needs of some particular segment within the parent population (such as choosing a Jewish school for your child, facing the Bar/Bat Mitzvah trauma, talking about God with kids, a single parents' shmooze, adoption and the Jewish family and ritual and family life).

- *Surprises.* One of the advantages of a five- or six-day retreat is the flexibility to adjust the program when an issue emerges from the group. Preparation before the retreat is critical, but there are many things you cannot possibly know beforehand. For example, you may not know in advance who your single parents are. You could hazard a guess—the application may list one adult, but there will be parents who come alone because a spouse cannot get vacation, there are often single parents who come with one of their own parents, and so on. Other issues will emerge from the chemistry of the parents and kids and program and staff. Part of the job of directing such a program is to be alert to these issues as they emerge and then to shape the program accordingly (within the limits of the remaining time).

For a Weekend Retreat
  These activities offer a blending of the two kinds of study.
- *First-night parents' evening program.* As in the description for the first night of a longer retreat (p. 54).

- *Shabbat morning study/Parashat HaShavua (the Torah reading).* After morning tefilla, the children go off with their counselors for group activities and the parents gather for study. In the settings I have worked in, commitment to traditional text study has determined the general focus of the study session in this time slot. I have always seen this as an opportunity to provide a taste of the kind of exciting, intellectually challenging Jewish experience that we can provide with a daily study session in a longer retreat. At the same time, because of the paucity of "adult time" available on a forty-eight-hour retreat, I have always felt the pressure to make the time go twice as far. For this reason I have tried to make this Parashat haShavua session also be a session about family. In considering the week's parasha, I have always tried to choose a selection that yields the possibility of meeting both goals. For example, Parashat Terumah (Exodus 25:1–27:19) deals with the building of the *Mishkan* (temporary place of worship in the desert). On the weekend for which this was the Torah reading, we studied a section of the parasha itself and then looked at midrashim (commentary in the form of teaching stories) that compare the building of the Mishkan to the building of a home. When we had a retreat on the Shabbat of Parashat Emor (Leviticus 21:1–24:23), which details the Jewish holidays, we talked about the influence of the calendar on our lives and the conflict inherent in living in a world in which the secular-Christian calendar shapes and even dictates the pace of our lives while we struggle to live (in many different ways) by the Jewish calendar.

- *Shabbat afternoon.* On Shabbat afternoon we always offer a choice between what we call Shabbat 101 and a text study session. The choice is offered for several reasons. First of all, it respects the different concerns and interests that the participants bring with them. Shabbat 101 is designed to answer any and all questions that parents have about bringing Shabbat into their homes (or extending or reinforcing it). There are always some participants who are satisfied with their family's current Shabbat celebration and do not feel the need to explore this further. Other families may not be particularly interested in Shabbat as an expression of their family's Jewishness. There are also parents for whom the opportunity for the more intellectual experience of text exploration is one of the main attractions of a retreat. The opportunity to choose a study session empowers parents' Jewishness by enabling them to make choices in line with their personal interests.

    I usually begin Shabbat 101 by asking, "What would you like to talk about?" I then go wherever the group wants within the broader topic of Shabbat. This discussion almost always wends its way to encompass two different but closely related areas of need for families: helps, hints and how-to information related to the practical aspects of taking what I call "the baby steps" in Jewish observance; and reinforcement and encouragement for the Jewish journey composed of these baby steps. (I come with some handouts and texts but most of the time I do not use them.) I answer questions but usually only after group members have made suggestions to one another. Here are questions that typify the two needs:

"But what do you *do* that's *special* that children can understand on Friday night?" Another participant answers, "Well, after Steve and I finished our 'Introduction to Judaism' class, we decided to use our wedding china, which we'd only used on Thanksgiving, for Friday night. After a few weeks we decided that we would turn the TV off during dinner on Friday night. A few weeks after that we decided to eat Friday night dinner in the dining room. Now it feels like a party every Friday night and it's fun. Josh (three years old) loves it!"

"But if I keep my children home on Friday night, aren't I robbing them of being part of the mainstream culture they live in?" I try to reassure parents that we all have this worry but that in the long run, their children live in that culture the rest of the week and can be as immersed as we want them to be. To miss out on Shabbat is to rob them of something more precious. Shabbat and the protected family time it offers is something only parents can provide, and only now. I almost always wrap up with the poem "The Generations" by Antoine de St. Exupery (p. 185). There is rarely a dry eye in the group.

"Who here is trying to raise your kid with more Jewishness than you were raised with?" Parents are looking for guidelines to help them in an area in which they are novices. The knowledge that almost everyone in the group (often including staff) is in the same boat is helpful.

- *Sunday morning—a chance to talk about "family stuff."* this session is usually slotted for an hour and a half. I have used Sentence Stubs and paragraphs as described above (p. 54). I have also used a third type of activity, which I call Dilemmas. In this activity each participant gets an index card and a pencil with which to write a Jewish family dilemma or question he could use some advice about. Everyone's card is dropped in the hat, and then the hat is passed so that everyone draws one. We go around the table (or circle), and each problem is read aloud with no comments. Then we have a chance to comment on what we have heard. Usually the problems fall into recognizable categories. The immediate feeling is of tremendous bonding created by the honesty and openness—but also by the realization that everyone is seriously grappling with the complexities of creating a Jewish family life.

The discussion proceeds to give advice on each and every problem (or clump of problems). I try to encourage participants to make suggestions from their own perspectives, creativity and experience. I add mine as well, but only when participants have given theirs (or if the group seems stumped or needs a push). The session always goes up to and over its time limit and is very hard to bring to closure. I think this happens because this kind of discussion is what parents really come for and what they really need. Someone always says, "Why did we wait until we're almost ready to leave to get into this? We should have started with this on

Friday night." Of course, they do not realize that they would not have been ready to share so deeply or receive so meaningfully when they had barely met.

Music and Singing

Music is one of the critical building blocks of a retreat because it is one of the major ambience- and community-building factors. In addition, careful selection of songs can enhance and reinforce the "message" of the retreat.

New songs. We always chose four or five songs for teaching during a forty-eight hour retreat, trying to select one or two related to the theme (for example, Debbie Friedman's "Lechi Lach" for a Shabbat whose parasha is Lech Lecha or "Make Those Waters Part" for a Shabbat concentrating on the Exodus or before Pesach) as well as songs that reflect a balance of English and Hebrew and of length and accessibility of melody. (Hit parade favorites have included "Hava NaShira," "The Family Song," Craig Taubman's "V'Shinantam," and "V'Anachnu N'Varech Ya". See p. 222 for music sources.)

Informal singing, drawing on those American/preschool/camp all-time favorites that most families know. We use music as a way to gather people for our next large group event. It focuses everyone and creates group feeling as people are arriving, settling in and transitioning from their previous activity. Whether you are gathering in a circle on the floor or outside on the rocks and grass, music works to collect everyone. Good songs to use for this purpose include songs in which individual kids and parents can add a verse (such as "Waterside," in which each kid can add something he or she saw down by the waterside) and those that are common knowledge (such as "Take Me Out to the Ball Game" and "She'll Be Coming 'Round the Mountain"), as well as some simple, widely known Hebrew songs ("Oseh Shalom") and *niggunim* (songs with few or no words). The selection will vary with the age range and backgrounds of your campers.

More-formal singing sessions. It is nice to have set times for group singing. These sessions are a bit more formal in structure than the singing-while-gathering sessions. It is during these times that the song leader will teach a new song, review a new song and lead other songs that can be sung with the help of a songbook. For example, "The Mishpaha Song" and "The Alef-Bet Song" do not really need to be taught. Everyone catches on to these fast, but it helps to be able to refer to the words on a poster or a songsheet or songbook.

Enhancement of tefilla (accompaniment on guitar). The addition of guitar accompaniment to tefilla seems to fill in the space and lift voices. Having some simple guitar music in the background during quiet, reflective moments enhances the mood.

However, it is important to stress that tefilla and singing should be distinct experiences for participants. These two areas have a large overlap. Both are strong community experiences. Many of the best-known Hebrew songs are drawn from the prayerbook. This overlap is all the more reason for care in the creation of the desired mood for each. Select songs, prayers and melodies so that each has its own texture and mood. Tefilla should not feel like a song session. Music can enhance the tefilla experience but should not overpower it.

Two additional aspects need to be considered in planning the music program:

Closing circle/closing program. The closing program should always incorporate music. Singing of the songs shared by the families during the retreat is an important aspect of the closure participants need before saying good-bye. Over the years we have included two kinds of "good-bye music" as well. On our shorter and smaller (fifteen to twenty families) retreat, we have always chosen a good-bye song in which everyone can easily learn the song's chorus. Each family's name is then made part of the song so that as we sing it, we go around the circle and sing a separate good-bye to each family as they have a moment in the spotlight. With a longer retreat and larger group, we usually compose a family camp song (see p. 195).

Shabbat. On a retreat which does *not* begin on Friday afternoon, it is possible to create a musical component to Erev Shabbat, which enhances Shabbat for everyone and adds at least one song to the repertoire of most of the group. Each group of kids, and the adults as a group, can learn a song to sing to the whole community at Kabbalat Shabbat or during the Oneg Shabbat. The kids can learn their song with the song leader while they are with their counselors, and the adults can learn their song before or after their study session. Each group knows that they are preparing a surprise presentation for the rest of the group. It also works to have everyone learn different melodic parts of the same song, to be sung together in harmony at the beginning of Shabbat.

No matter when your retreat begins, you can schedule time for "The Great Havdalah Choir." This can be a Shabbat afternoon activity or about half an hour at which everyone learns the Klepper-Friedlander song "Shavua Tov! May You Have a Good Week" along with another quiet Havdalah-mood song.

Tefilla

One of the gifts that a retreat setting is most able to provide for a family is that of prayer. The receptivity of people to new experiences, which a retreat seems to bring about, creates the doorway to this experience. Whether the tefilla you fashion is a few minutes long or comes closer to a full traditional service, the family can be refreshed and nurtured by the experience of strengthened links to community, the expression of appreciation for the many gifts received, the restoration of perspective, the time for communion with God, for quiet reflection and for celebration of the start of a new day. In addition, this kind of prayer experience begins to chip away at the loneliness and separateness that individuals and families often feel, by linking family members more tightly to one another, to the other families, to the extended community of the Jewish people and to God.

All the practical details and decisions flow from this. You should decide what kind of prayer experience you want to provide for your retreat, given the framework of the sponsoring agency and taking into consideration the age range and distribution of the children who will be there, the background of the adults who will be there (to the extent that you can know this in advance) and the type and flexibility of the space you have available for tefilla.

Question. What are the givens of your sponsoring agency? Is your retreat/camp under the auspices of a synagogue? A community central agency? A school? A havurah?

A synagogue will usually have some sort of framework related to the movement of which you are a part. A school or central agency may have a set of standards for community events. In either case, get a clear statement of the bottom line relative to prayer.

Question. Will you include a service on Friday evening? Shabbat morning? Shabbat afternoon? Sunday/weekday morning?

Question. Are there particular prayers which must be included?

- Does Shabbat morning have to include a Torah reading? A telling of the week's Torah reading? Neither? A haftarah reading?

- If Torah reading is a given, how much must be read?

- What will/can be the participation of non-Jews in the service?

- Is there a particular prayerbook that you are committed to using? If you have a choice, what are the available options?

- What are the guidelines for the use of musical instruments or taped music on Shabbat and during prayer?

In planning tefilla for a retreat, it is important to keep in mind that prayer is not part of most families' daily or even weekly routine.

It is not an arena in which most of them will have found a comfortable form of Jewish expression.

For these reasons it is important to create a prayer environment that is as inviting and nonthreatening as possible. Look for a space in which participants can sit in a circle or semicircle or in concentric circles. In some spaces adults might be seated on chairs and kids on carpet squares on the floor. At Ramah, where we had a very large group and only benches were available for seating, our tefilla leader invented an arrangement which we came to call the "Wagon Wheel." In this setup the tefilla leader stood in the middle of the space, from which pairs of benches set close together radiated outward. Families were asked to sit close together and facing one another so that they were knee to knee and shoulder to shoulder and quite cozy. We removed all extra benches so that the entire group was close, and we arranged to have too few prayerbooks and prayer pages so families had to share. This all worked to create physical closeness for the group, which helped to bring about the community mood that this tefilla leader sought. The arrangement of the room can announce to people, even before things begin, that this will be a different kind of prayer experience.

As people walk in, there should be a siddur* and tefilla sheets for those old enough to read, with sung-out-loud prayers in transliteration, keyed to the pages in the siddur itself and designed for those of all ages who do not read Hebrew (see p. 198).

Try for a warm, relaxed but quiet and reflective mood. Begin with some quiet singing, the kind that requires no words (other than "la-la-la") or includes songs kids may have learned in preschool or religious school ("Shabbat Shalom" and "Mah Yafeh HaYom") or that most people have some familiarity with ("Oseh Shalom"). Encourage people to move and sway and put their arms around their family members.

Kabbalat Shabbat

If your retreat will begin on Friday, with participants arriving until sundown and Kabbalat Shabbat scheduled before dinner, it is important to set modest goals for Kabbalat Shabbat. The participant families will not have become a community yet, and successful group tefilla is an expression of community togetherness. A group of strangers newly arrived in a new setting is not yet a community.

It will help to get everything off the ground if Kabbalat Shabbat can begin with some kind of structured "hello saying" (say hi to the person sitting in front of you or Shabbat Shalom to the person nearest to you whom you have not yet met). However, this will not create community by itself. Because people have had to pack and travel and unpack (and the population includes many young children), it is important to get to dinner as quickly as possible. This is not the time for more complete or complex getting-to-know-you games.

I have always found that the process of becoming a community just takes time, and therefore although Kabbalat Shabbat on the first night of a retreat can be very nice, it never feels quite the way I wish it to. It takes dinner together (with assigned seats) and some singing and games and dancing for people to begin to feel comfortable and for connections between them to begin to grow. Of course, the situation is quite different if your retreat begins even as early as Thursday. In that case, the community you have worked hard to bring into being may actually be able to celebrate Shabbat as a community.

A suggested Kabbalat Shabbat

Opening: Quiet singing ("Shabbat Shalom," "Mah Yafeh HaYom"); a short Shabbat story or short welcoming talk (three sentences) about joining together to welcome Shabbat.

Lecha Dodi (at least the first and last verses)

Mizmor Shir L'Yom HaShabbat

Barekhu

The *Maariv Aravim* paragraph in English

The *Ohev Amo Yisrael* blessing

The opening sentence of the *Shma* and the *Ve Ahavta* paragraph

(Depending on time, attention span and age range: Debbie Friedman's English version of *Ve Ahavta*, "And You Shall Love the Lord Your God")

Hashkivenu in English

The first three berakhot of the *Amidah* (sung aloud together)

Quiet time for personal prayer: We sometimes have those who wish to do so, continue on with the *Amidah* silently, while the kids gather (this works best if they are on the floor) close to the leader who asks them to think of some things they would like to thank God for, which they then share in whispers; it is also nice to have some quiet guitar music in the background.

Shalom Rav (or *Oseh Shalom* to a tune most people know)

Alenu

Kaddish

"Mah Yafeh HaYom" (or other closing song)

Shaharit*

Every spiritual tradition has its way of greeting the new day. Family camp is a wonderful setting in which to introduce families to Shaharit—our morning tefilla. The time to sit together for a few minutes of music and hugs, quiet reflection and gratitude for God's blessings is a powerfully centering experience with which to meet a new day. The mood and activity of Shaharit offer a contrast to the rushed morning routine most families experience at home. Here, poised between breakfast and activity, the family can linger and the community can connect before the hubbub of the day.

This is a high-energy time of day. Your Shaharit can harness this energy with music, mime and even dance. Include a story. Use rhythm instruments. Tell a short story.

A Suggested Shaharit

Some singing as people gather: "Mah Yafeh HaYom," "Halleluyah," "Hinay Mah Tov"

Modeh Ani

Mah Tovu

Ashrei: Leader and congregation alternatively sing in Hebrew or read in English, or sing the last line (*Va'Anachnu*) using the Craig Taubman melody or the Debbie Friedman melody.

Halleluyah (Psalm 150): Sing; children can mime the various instruments; you might actually want to involve use of different rhythm instruments for this prayer.

Barekhu

Or Hadash

V'Ha'er Eynenu: Traditional melody or the Debbie Friedman melody

Shma: Chant the first paragraph together. Read the second paragraph silently or out loud together. Chant the third paragraph and explain about the *tzitzit*, the fringes in the corners of the *tallit*.* Share the tzitzit around so everyone gets to kiss them. You can also choose to sing Debbie Friedman's version of the first paragraph in English and Craig Taubman's *V'Shinantam*.

Mikhamokha

Amidah: Sing the first three berakhot out loud. Leave quiet time for people to read the rest quietly or meditate or pray personal prayers while the kids gather close (as described in the preceding section on Kabbalat Shabbat). It is also nice to have some quiet guitar music in the background.

Conclude with *Oseh Shalom*.

Torah Service (on Shabbat, Monday and Thursday; see below)

Musaf* (on Shabbat; see below)

Alenu

Kaddish

Adon Olam: Let some older kids who know it choose a melody and lead it.

Torah Service

Some Torah songs

Ki MiTziyon

March around with the Torah so everyone can kiss it.

Read from the Torah (or tell the story depending on your choice): The traditional pattern is three *aliyot** on a weekday and seven on Shabbat. It is nice to give each *aliyah** (opportunity to go up to the Torah) to one family. Variations: Give an aliyah to people who have birthdays or other special occasions in the weeks surrounding the retreat; each age-group of children can come up for an aliyah with their counselors saying the berakhot and the parents holding a large tallit over them; at one weekend Shabbat Camp we "named" a five-year-old who had never received a Hebrew name.

V'Zot haTorah

Have participants join in "dressing" the Torah after the reading.

On Shabbat: Read the *haftarah** (prophetic reading that complements the week's Torah portion).

March around with the Torah.

Etz Hayim

Musaf. If your group is still focused enough to continue, Musaf is actually just the addition of another *Amidah* (do in similar fashion to the Shaharit *Amidah*) and *Ein Kelohenu* (very easy to learn and sing) before *Alenu*.

HaMotzi and Birkat haMazon
     The tradition of reciting a berakha before and after meals offers a three-times-a-day opportunity to explore the world of prayer. A berakha is an acknowledgement of a gift. The berakhot before and after meals acknowledge the gift of food. The challenge is to teach the berakhot so that people become comfortable with the rote aspect of the ritual but also master a way of maintaining meaning within the rote.

The berakha we refer to as *haMotzi* is probably among the most familiar berakhot to Jews from all kinds of backgrounds. For this reason it is very easily fitted into the flow of the camp/retreat experience. There are always children who are thrilled to take responsibility for leading the recitation or singing of the berakha. The easiest way to help this happen is to start each meal by having everyone find a seat. Have sliced bread, rolls or breadsticks on each table so that everyone may take some bread in hand and recite the blessing together. After this start, tables may proceed to the buffet table.

Birkat haMazon presents two obstacles: it is unfamiliar to many and it is long. Your halakhic framework will guide you here in terms of how much you are required to include. At the minimum, it is important to provide some attention to the idea of thankfulness for the food we have eaten. This can be structured in a range of ways, from recitation of the entire Birkat haMazon to a moment of silence. I suggest trying each of those extremes at least once but choosing a middle path for most of your meals. The entire Birkat haMazon can be very overwhelming for people who are not already familiar with it. Rather than encouraging people to learn, it can actually become a discouraging experience. A weekend retreat does not include enough meals to provide mastery.

I have always tried to set a middle-of-the-road pattern and then vary it. The variation serves to remind people what the prayer is all about and also to provide an alternative model that they might take home and incorporate into their family meals. The pattern that seems to work best is to use one of the abridged versions of Birkat haMazon.[5] I ask the counselors and staff to sing loudly and clearly so that people can be guided by their voices and sing along with them.

A weekend retreat only includes six meals, and so we stick with this pattern for all six meals. People do actually begin to catch on and join in. On a longer encampment I use this pattern for the first four or five meals and then break the pattern by asking everyone to read it together in English or read it privately in silence. We return to the pattern of singing Birkat haMazon as a group for a meal or two and then break it again by reading a story or midrash about food and its value to us (p. 176). Sometimes I allow a minute of silence for people to say their own thank-you to God in their own way.

At the end of the retreat, we give everyone copies of the version of Birkat haMazon that we have been reciting to take home with them. After some retreats we have made tapes for participants

---

[5]Among versions that I have used:

UJA Book of Songs and Blessings (New York: United Jewish Appeal, 1982). The booklet contains long (traditional) and abridged versions in Hebrew along with transliteration and English.

CCAR Table Version of Birkat HaMazon (New York: Central Conference of American Rabbis, 1987). Sold as a set of three along with the Erev Shabbat table blessings and Havdalah; includes Hebrew, English, transliteration and musical score.

Kol Haneshama, Songs and Grace after Meals (Wyncote, Pa.: Reconstructionist Press, 1991). Includes traditional version and creative abridged versions in Hebrew and English with some transliteration.

with songs we have sung. We always include the chanting of Birkat haMazon on the tape as well.

Something else to think about: Younger children are often finished eating and getting restless just as their parents are halfway through food and conversation. We invented a system that enabled kids to leave the table and play safely while parents enjoyed the luxury of lingering over their food and conversation. The system was "mealtime shmirah." This involved assigning counselors (usually two but sometimes more, depending on the number of children, the physical layout and the weather) to supervise free play.

About fifteen minutes after the meal began, counselors took up stations (outside the dining room on the lawn, on the patio or in some area inside the dining room). When the children saw the counselors get up, those who were finished eating joined them for supervised play while the adults finished the meal. Activities ranged from reading stories to lawn games such as Duck-duck-goose, frisbee or jump rope. As the meal drew to a close, someone would call all the children to come and sit down again with their families for Birkat haMazon.

This system helped to make meals more enjoyable for all. It provided an ideal win-win situation for all family members. Children were free to play, and parents could linger over a meal in conversation with other adults. The structure helped make a statement about the importance of Birkat haMazon, reinforcing the halakhic framework of the retreat. It modeled clear behavior expectations and avoided the kind of negotiations that often characterize the "It's-time-to-stop-playing-and-come-in" interaction between parent and child.

Shabbat

"The seventh day is a palace in time which we build,"[6] and only the retreat setting (of all family education settings) offers its participants the experience of twenty-four hours in this palace. Only the retreat can create this complete, authentic, wrap-around Shabbat experience. From the intensity of this immersion in Shabbat, many families derive their commitment to take something of the experience home and inject it into their family life.

The program builds the palace in time for the families to enter, explore and experience. Its shape is in large part determined by the halakhic framework within which a particular retreat functions. Ideally, its contents are more inspiration and experience than instruction for several reasons. First of all, complete observance of Shabbat is made up of mastery of a myriad of details all of which could never be conveyed in one Shabbat. If the Shabbat program is concentrated on how-to instruction, it takes away from immersion in the experience for its own sake. How-to also divides those who know from those who do not know, which can have the effect of dividing the community into the "knows" and the "don't knows." And finally, it is

---

[6] Abraham Joshua Heschel, *The Sabbath* (Philadelphia: Jewish Publication Society, 1963), 14.

unlikely that people decide to light Shabbat candles simply because someone taught them the blessings, but people have been motivated to learn the blessings from the inspiration of a Shabbat experience.

These factors remain constant on any retreat but the actual nature of the "palace in time" varies greatly with whether Shabbat is at the beginning of the retreat (with families arriving just prior to Shabbat) or comes later in a longer retreat.

Each setting of Shabbat has its assets and liabilities. When a retreat begins with Shabbat, as weekend retreats do, Shabbat constitutes the bulk of the retreat. This means that many programming slots have to be designed to accomplish overlapping goals. As discussed above (p. 49), the Erev Shabbat program and the getting-to-know-you first night program become one, study of the parashat hashavua and discussion of family issues combine (p. 61), and much of the singing is organized around Shabbat. Beginning a retreat with Shabbat also provides the challenge of molding a community and celebrating community at the same time. As we pointed out in the tefilla section, it is for this reason that the first few hours will always feel a bit awkward. Shabbat is a celebration of community. People who have just arrived and have barely met each other cannot yet be a community. In a longer retreat, Shabbat can come at a mid-point or later in the retreat and provide the experience of community celebration.

In a retreat beginning with Shabbat, bonds between people are being built as Shabbat progresses, and the fine details of the program are designed to guide this process along. When Shabbat is celebrated later in the retreat, it becomes a day for enjoying the bonds which have emerged during the week. For this reason, Shabbat on a weekend retreat will be more programmed than Shabbat which is part of a longer encampment. During the latter, more unstructured time can be a feature of the program.

Many facets of Shabbat programming have already been covered in the preceding discussions of getting the program going, study, tefilla and music. I reserve the rest of this chapter for those things relating to the building of that "palace in time" which have not been covered elsewhere.

Expectations. Families arrive at a retreat with very different expectations about what Shabbat is or will be. It helps everyone when the halakhic framework for the retreat is clearly stated so that expectations, *do's* and *don'ts* are explicit. On a weekend retreat, we put some of this succinctly into our memo to parents (p. 155) and also give out a short hand-out about Shabbat (p. 171). For family camp we gave out a similar Shabbat memo on Friday morning.

Preparations. Some of the specialness of Shabbat comes from the extensive preparations that go into it. It is the way the "palace in time" gets built. As families arrive on Friday afternoon, have one or two easy projects that involve them in this preparation in an informal way. Several successful activities that can be used this way: a big butcher-paper wall hanging prepared with Shabbat Shalom written in huge outline letters so children and grownups can color and decorate it; some kind of table-decoration project—decorating paper tablecloths, making pipe cleaner flower centerpieces, decorating small flowerpots and planting plants; setting the dinner tables. All of these can absorb families as they arrive and also provide a natural setting for beginning to talk and make connections as people color and create.

On a longer retreat, preparation can of course be more extensive. If it is at all possible, have the families make their own loaves of hallah from prepared dough. At Ramah, where there is a chef to attend to this, we have done it with dough prepared in the kitchen. At a retreat site where this was not possible, we bought hallah dough (packed in one-loaf hunks of dough to each plastic bag) in the city and brought it along with us to camp.

The children's groups should spend part of their time on Friday making some kind of special Shabbat preparations. These often include similar activities to those mentioned above, along with more time-intensive projects such as decorated paper placemats, tie-dyed hallah covers, mobiles to hang from the dining room ceiling, vases filled with wildflowers collected around camp, brownies or cookies baked for dessert or for Kiddush the next day, new *kippot* (plain satin or cloth decorated with puffy pens), rolled colorful beeswax candles and the "Shabbat-a-gram" project mentioned in the tzedakah section (p. 71). Depending on the talents of your specialists and counselors, each group can learn a dance or song or skit (or all three) to present at some time during Shabbat.

Parents' preparation for Shabbat can fall into similar programming areas. Parents can make havdalah candles or baskets for hallot or flowers. They can learn a song or dance to present to the children at some point during Shabbat. And we usually offer parents some additional pre-Shabbat study sessions, such as learning how to say Kiddush in one hour, studying a selection from *The Sabbath* by Heschel, "Shabbat with Training Wheels" (Shabbat for beginners—come with all your questions) and "Create a Shabbat Choir."

Wearing white clothing (or as much white as possible) helps create a special atmosphere. This can work if you have requested in precamp correspondence that people bring white clothes.

Candlelighting. Have all the candles set up on one table in the dining room. Ask people in advance to bring their own candlesticks, but be ready to provide some, using heavy weight foil pans or heavy-weight glass ashtrays. Gathering the community around the candle-set table can create a magical mood. Ask people to stand with their families. Set a mood with quiet songs. It helps to set aside thirty seconds of silence for everyone to think back on something special they want to remember from the past week. Join together to sing or say the blessings. (Be sure there are lots of hand-outs with the words in Hebrew, transliteration and English.) It helps maintain the mood during the transition to tefilla if you can accompany the change of place with the singing of some Shabbat songs.

Erev Shabbat table blessings. After tefilla, maintain the mood with singing again as all return to the dining room and find their assigned seats (p. 48). Each table should have a hand-out for every parent with the texts (in Hebrew, transliteration and English) for "Shalom Aleikhem," the parental blessing of the children, Kiddush, hand washing and hallah.[7] Guide people through this with the briefest explanations possible, followed by recitation of the blessings in unison.

Daytime details. To get a feeling for variations of Shabbat programming, look at the three different Shabbat schedules in the Hand-outs section (pp. 149 and 166). In the longer family camp format, Shabbat afternoon is turned over more completely to families to spend on their own as they choose. There are totally open unstructured times, and there are slots with activities available for those families seeking some structure. On a weekend retreat, the afternoon tends to be divided into family time and group time. On a short retreat, we use part of Shabbat afternoon for adult study time. The children spend the latter half of the afternoon in Shabbat activities with their counselors.

Havdalah. Shabbat ends with Havdalah. When it turns dark at about six, we follow Havdalah with the making of spiceboxes—the message being that the spiceboxes are to take home and use for Havdalah next week. Spicebox making is followed by Family Fun Night (p. 114). When the end of Shabbat is closer to eight or so, a Shabbat version of Family Fun Night will precede Havdalah, and spiceboxes will be made as part of Sunday's program.

Havdalah works well when members of the group stand close together in a circle (or in concentric circles) with arms around one another. Set the mood with a quiet song or two. Provide a one-sentence explanation of Havdalah and an additional sentence about the wine, spices and candles. Chant clearly and close by singing "Shavua Tov" with the traditional melody. We usually have our song leader lead us with the song "Shavua Tov, May You Have a Good Week," which has a very easily learned chorus which we sing while she sings the verses. Participants are then initiated into the "family camp custom" of finding seven new friends made this weekend (or week) and wishing them each *Shavua Tov.**

---

[7]The ideal version for our purposes is the table booklet accompanying Ron Wolfson's *The Shabbat Seder*, which is part of The Art of Jewish Living Series (New York: Federation of Jewish Men's Clubs, 1985). The CCAR three-fold mentioned in footnote 5 of this chapter is also useful here.

We hope that the Shabbat experience a family shares at a retreat will send them home rested, nourished and feeling better about themselves as a family. If this happens to even a small degree, they will seek to recreate it for themselves by introducing some Shabbat at home. This is more likely to happen if we can send home with them some of the tools they need—the hand-outs used in camp for the blessings, the words to the songs, a tape with the songs and blessings, a Shabbat story to read next week, two candles for next week, a spicebox . . . . These tangible take-home items, along with their memories of the camp Shabbat and the traces of the good feelings they bring home, become the tools for each family to begin to seek out Shabbat experiences in their community and build their own version of the "palace in time."

Tzedakah[8]

It is important to include some kind of tzedakah programming in each retreat. This is an activity that all participants can join in regardless of their background. People value it as a family endeavor. It is something families can continue to be involved in at home without acquiring any new skills or knowledge. This is more easily accomplished during an encampment longer than forty-eight hours but can be squeezed in during a shorter retreat as well.

At a weekend retreat, families can be asked to bring some money to put in a tzedakah box prior to Shabbat. (If people are notified before the weekend, they can set aside some pennies in advance or decide on a sum their family would like to give to tzedakah.) This could be followed up with a story about tzedakah, read at the Friday evening Oneg Shabbat or at a Shabbat afternoon storytelling activity. The story could even be given out in photocopied form for families to read together at bedtime.

After Havdalah or on Sunday morning, families can make tzedakah boxes to take home with them. Children can count the money collected on Erev Shabbat, wrap it in coin rolls (which can be bought ready-made) and decide where to donate it.

On retreats where we bought and prepared our own food, we always arranged to give whatever was left over and perishable to a local food bank. We involved one or two families in taking responsibility for delivering the food.

One summer at Ramah Family Camp, we asked families to save the pennies left in their pockets at the end of the day during the month preceding camp for a *tikkun olam** project (p. 136). On the second day of camp we announced that lunch was the time to bring the family "penny harvest" to the dining room. We set up a card table in the dining room with a glass container and asked people to pour in their family's pennies as they entered. The amazement,

---

*Contribution of money to help make the world a better place.

enthusiasm and pride of the children as they added their family pennies to the group collection was contagious.

The process of combining the pennies helped build community in a deeply powerful but unexpected way. We had originally invited people to bring pennies if they wanted to. Families brought widely varying amounts but felt a stake in the whole. The whole was clearly far greater than the sum of the parts. And the sheer quantity was very mesmerizing for the children.

From this flowed a series of activities: We had a contest for guessing the amount of money. (The winner was announced at the closing celebration.) All the children participated in counting the money. Older groups packed the pennies in penny rolls. The oldest group took responsibility for deciding what use to make of the money. In one session the oldest group actually led a campaign for four different causes, conducted a vote and then divided the pennies proportionally among the causes to reflect the popular vote.

Families or children can become involved while at camp in doing something to raise money for tzedakah. They can make and sell popcorn or wash cars. They can get sponsorship for swimming or running laps, hula-hooping or bouncing a ball. At Ramah it is traditional to raise money for tzedakah by selling "Shabbat-a-grams" on Friday afternoon. A "Shabbat-a-gram" is a "Shabbat Shalom" greeting card sent by a friend. The group in charge makes the cards and sets up a table at which they are sold on Friday afternoon. The buyer adds a personal greeting, the card is stapled closed and addressed to the recipient. The cards are delivered shortly before Shabbat. The money earned is allocated by the group in charge.

Children's Program

An important part of the total family experience is the quality of the time each family member spends with her peers. While the parents are engaged in study, discussion, tennis, sunbathing or free time, the children are enjoying time in their own age-groups with their counselors.

Age-Groups

One of the most challenging aspects of organizing a family retreat is that, in sharp distinction to camp or school, you cannot predict what ages and sexes and concentrations of both you will end up with. Although you may have a tentative framework for age-grouping, the actual formation of groups has to wait until your registration is substantial or complete. As a result, you should delay assigning your staff to specific age-groups and even on your staff meeting until the shape of the kids' groupings has emerged.

In terms of social and intellectual needs, it makes sense to strive for a preschool group (ages two through four) that can be further subdivided if necessary, plus groups that take in (approximately) ages five and six, seven and eight, nine through eleven, and twelve through fourteen. Needless to say, this may be much modified by your actual registration, as well as by the distribution of the sexes of the kids. (A group with one seven-year-old girl and six six-year-old boys will not work well for the girl, whereas this is not a factor for two-year-olds.) On one retreat, we saw that we had only one twelve-year-old girl; the kids nearest to her age were four ten-year-old boys. We called her parents and suggested that she bring a friend, which she did. This worked out well.

Other information about the kids can have an impact on group formation. For example, at one retreat a mature twelve-year-old girl with cerebral palsy fit better with a slightly younger group (tens and elevens), which was going to do more activities in which she could participate, than with her own age group, which was mostly soccer-crazy boys. The Hand-outs section contains several different age-group lists (p. 151).

Program Design

The rough outlines of the program design will be determined by your overall schedule and by the weather and the site. The weather will affect the possibilities for outdoor and indoor activities and swimming. The layout and facilities of the site will influence such factors as sports, games, hikes and crafts.

In designing a day of children's programming for a family retreat or camp, I have found that a helpful rule of thumb is to select activities that stand out from the routine kinds of school/camp stuff so that the retreat activities feel special and memorable for children (and parents). I think it is important that experiences take advantage of the setting and the community. As a corollary to this, I never use videotapes in children's programming. (They watch enough—too much?—at home and in school.)

Select from the following list of elements:

Something Jewish. Kids should experience meaningful Jewish study as part of their family camp experience. This can take many forms. It should feel different from school but substantial.

On a weekend program, kids might do any of the following:

- Hear a version of the week's Torah portion and act out the story.

- Participate in a "Torah Roll": A Torah scroll is unrolled as far as possible and children learn about what is in a Torah scroll and how it is written; they have an opportunity to use a Torah pointer, look for letters, look at the stitching and participate in rerolling and dressing the Torah afterward. Complementary activities for later in the day or the next day: Torah paper doll;[9] origami Torah scroll; a chance to try quill, ink and parchment.

---

[9] Kit #1 in the *Together* series; see chapter 1, footnote 1.

- Hear a Shabbat story, complemented with a related craft activity. (This is most likely to duplicate a Jewish school experience.)
- Hear a tzedakah story and follow up the next day with a tzedakah-raising activity such as a hula-hoop-a-thon or a jump-a-thon; make tzedakah boxes.

On a longer retreat, the children's program can include a daily forty-five-minute discussion in which they follow something through in several segments. At Ramah Family Camp the content of the children's discussion sessions paralleled the content of the adults' study sessions.

Something active. It is a good idea to concentrate more on games than on sports. Mixed age and mixed sex groups do not work very well for serious sports. In addition, games, especially "new games" that are the collaborative, everybody-who-plays-wins type, send a different message about what is fun in a community. Include classic games like Hide and Seek, Freeze Tag and Red Light/Green Light that can be played anywhere, require no supplies and are fun for all. Avoid games that require blindfolds (many kids are frightened when they are blindfolded) and Red Rover (which can get too rough). Dancing and hiking fall into this active category, too.

Some kind of outdoor/nature activity. One of the features of being at camp is living close to nature. This is an asset to be taken advantage of. Is there a hike to a special place that is suitable for an older group? Is there some kind of nature hunt or search that combines looking, noticing and learning all at the same time? Can you collect bugs or leaves? Taking a walk to a secluded spot and then reading an ecology-oriented book such as *The Lorax* by Dr. Suess, *Just a Dream* by Chris Van Allsburg or *Miss Rumphius* by Barbara Cooney (see resource list, p. 221) can lead to a thought-provoking discussion. Try a "microhike": take a walk to a secluded spot and give everyone a length of string or yarn (twelve to eighteen inches long) to stretch out anywhere they wish. Give each child a magnifying glass to look closely at everything along the string. What/how many/how much can they notice? (The family nature activities described on page 120 may be adaptable for the children if they are not used for a family activity at another point in the retreat.)

A crafts activity. This type of activity does not require a specialist—just some preplanning of something your counselors can lead themselves. Crafts are easily combined with your "something Jewish" category as campers make Shabbat, Havdalah or Hanukkah candles (older campers); spiceboxes; tzedakah boxes; mezuzot*; decorated pillowcases for reclining at the seder; or origami Torah scrolls or flowers for the Shabbat table. Other successful crafts activities we have seen include Fimo pins or pendants for Mother's

Day (at a Shabbat Camp that took place over Mother's Day), friendship bracelets and tie-dyed T-shirts, socks and hallah covers.

An ideal camp activity is one that combines crafts with an activity such as making frisbees (plastic aquarium tubing and decorated paper plates), kites or paper airplanes. The creation of the play object is collegial, with counselors and kids sitting and working together, talking, laughing, singing or listening to music. Following this, everyone has a chance to enjoy playing with and using what has been made.

Music, dance and drama. If you have specialists or counselors who can lead these activities, they can provide the highlight of a retreat experience. Music, dance and drama can also be combined with the "something Jewish" category and often work well if the kids prepare something to present at Kabbalat Shabbat, the closing circle or morning services.

Cooking/baking. This can also combine with the "something Jewish" category. Kids can make hallah or bake brownies for Kiddush. They can bake the birthday cake for someone celebrating a birthday. At one Shabbat Camp, which took place two weeks before Passover, each group of kids prepared a different kind of haroset from a different Jewish ethnic group.

Sheer fun. Bubble blowing (p. 187).

Family Choices

Some families choose to spend extra time together and decide to use what would be group time as additional family time. *This is a good thing!* After all, we are promoting *family* education. However, parents need to know that although we encourage this, they have a responsibility to inform the counselors when a child will be missing from the group so that counselors do not have to go looking for a "missing" camper or spend valuable group time waiting for a camper they are expecting.

This is often a difficult aspect of family camp for counselors to accept, especially if they have prior experience with summer camp or youth groups, in which children's participation is assumed (mandatory). The counselors have put energy into planning a good program, and it can feel personal when a child (or family) opts out. Discuss this with counselors so they understand that a family's choosing to take a hike or fly a kite during group time is a sign of the camp's success.

Things to Save

If you are going to be seriously involved in family retreats (or any family education at all), the following things are useful to collect and save during the year:

- Small containers for making spiceboxes: spice jars, film containers, six- or eight-ounce yogurt containers, toilet paper or paper towel rolls, little match boxes (the kind restaurants give out), shoulder pads (open, put cloves and stick cinnamon in, add yarn hair and "puffy paint" or button features)

- Miscellaneous containers for making tzedakah boxes: coffee cans, cottage cheese or salsa containers with lids

- Metal bottle caps for candlesticks or Hanukkah menorahs

- Single socks (the ones that did not spring a hole or get lost in the wash) for sock puppets

- Yarn for hair on sock puppets and shoulder-pad spiceboxes

- Scrap paper of various sizes and colors from printers

- Old wallpaper books from a decorating store

- Paint chips (the samples from paint store, which are great for collages); green ones for the Green Machine nature hike (p. 120)

- Wooden sticks for mixing paints (useful for handles on face puppets)

- Shirt cardboards

- Plastic buckets and scoops from detergent (the large buckets are great for mixing bubble-blowing solution; the buckets and scoops are good sand toys)

- Baby food jars, to make spiceboxes or Rosh HaShana honey jars

- Bed sheets no longer in use (good for sewing projects and banners)

- The plastic spools that gift ribbon comes on (great for friendship bracelets when decorated with stickers or glued-on beads)

8 Staffing

Role Models

If I had thought about role models for families at all before the first Ramah Family Camp in 1987, I probably would have assumed (somewhat naively) that my own family and some of the families with teenage children would provide the role models that younger families might have been looking for.

Not! (as current teenage jargon would express it).

I was astonished to observe that the role models for the participating families turned out to be the counselors who were guiding the children during group time; helping to lead singing, dancing and prayer and joining in celebration. Serendipity!

The first time I observed this phenomenon I was very surprised and pleased, although I did not realize the implication of what I was seeing. (My intuition about the kind of counselors we needed for a family camp had been on target, but initially this seemed all there was to it—that the parents liked the counselors and felt good about them.) It was when I saw it again at Family Camp the second summer and then at Shabbat Camp that I began to realize that something more than "liking the counselors" was going on. The recurrence and persistence of this phenomenon demanded that I look at it more closely.

Teenagers? Why teenagers? Why not families? Now that I have seen this process in action, it seems incredibly obvious. Our parents are struggling with raising their children to be good people and good Jews in a culture in which, in general, teenagers get bad press. Parents of young children see or hear the word teenager and think "sex, drugs and rock and roll" (the only exception perhaps being one wonderful babysitter or niece or nephew). Now they arrive at camp and see a crew of shiny, wholesome, enthusiastic, Jewishly interested and knowledgeable teens. Suddenly they begin to see a *model for the kind of people they would like their kids to grow up to be.*

And then they begin to ask the questions that have the potential to direct their own parenting decisions. Parents will often come up to me and ask, "Where did you find these wonderful teenagers?"

But more importantly, they begin to question the counselors themselves about their Jewishness, about the homes they grew up in, and about the Jewish education they received.

For the parents, these cross-generational encounters serve as conduits for the realization that the Jewish decisions they make along the way and the Jewish settings they provide for their children influence their children's emerging Jewish identity. On the one hand, these conversations make it clear that there is no one Jewish parenting "recipe." On the other hand, some striking similarities in the backgrounds of our counselors do emerge: for almost all, Jewish education (through high school) was a sine qua non, a nonnegotiable in their families. They went to various kinds of Jewish schools but do not recall having a choice about Jewish studies. Some of them recount fierce battles over this with unyielding parents, particularly in the post-Bar/Bat Mitzvah years. For a large proportion, Kashrut was a factor in their growing up—either their homes were kosher, or they returned from camp or youth group trying to persuade their parents to make their homes kosher, or they experimented with keeping kosher on their own. Most of them had a Jewish summer camp experience and some a Jewish youth group experience.

An interesting sidebar is that the conversations with parents are meaningful to the counselors too, often providing them a window on their own Jewish families, an opportunity to see their own Jewish experiences through another set of eyes. Things that they may not have noticed or may have taken for granted suddenly stand out in relief from the general mass of childhood and family "stuff." This is often an important threshold experience for moving into adulthood—a conversation with an adult who is not a parent, a relative or a family friend and, more importantly, who is genuinely interested in them and in what they have to say.

Programmatic Implications

The counselors are a critical part of the scaffolding—not only because they provide safety and fun for the children while the parents are engaged in adult programs but because of this issue of role models.

When this interest in the counselors has emerged publicly, it can be taken advantage of and woven into the programming of the retreat. Two case studies illustrate how we went about capturing this interest and making it part of the program:[1]

---

[1] Note that both examples are of programs that were spin-offs of scheduled "family stuff" programs. In both, the staff was able to pick up parents' interests, find time (in whatever time remained in the retreat) and create the format that would serve as the appropriate follow-through. In neither case was the spin-off part of the original program design. The staff read the signs and intuited what to do.

Case 1. After a tremendous success with the Sentence Stubs family program (see pp. 106), we felt the need to provide parents with a follow-up program for probing the issues that had raised the most interest. We designed a "Donahue Show"-type program[2] with a panel consisting of two Jewish educators (one male and one female), both of whom were parents; a single mother raising a nine-year-old son and an eleven-year-old daughter in a small city with a tiny Jewish community; a young father who had grown up in a totally assimilated community and was now involved in the Orthodox community; the mother of a family with four children (aged two, four, six and eight), which was the most observant family in its small suburban town; and two of the counselors—a young man who was entering his senior year in high school and a young woman entering her junior year at UCLA. Initially, questions were asked of everyone on the panel, but as the program developed, more and more questions began to be directed toward the two counselors. Parents were very clearly asking them for advice!

Most of these questions fell into two categories:[3] *limits*— what did their parents insist on (that is, make nonnegotiable)? and *personal consequences*—did they ever feel that they were missing out on something their friends were able to do while they were doing something Jewish? Both of these counselors came from families in which Jewish education through high school was a very definite nonnegotiable, and although each of them was able to recount examples of rebellion (passive or active), they knew they were only making a token test of something that had no give. With differing nuances, both of them expressed the observation that although there were times that the Jewishness of their families felt onerous, on balance they experienced family Jewish times as among their most positive family experiences.

Case 2. At one Family Camp, the Friday night Oneg Shabbat program for adults was an "Ask Our Rabbis" panel. The six panel members had all been members of the staff all week: two husband-and-wife rabbinic couples (one Reform and one Conservative), plus two additional Conservative rabbis. In planning the evening program, our assumption had been that people would have many miscellaneous questions about medical ethics and life cycle events and that this would be an interesting and even fun way to answer people's Jewish questions (we had lively panelists). The questions never touched any of those areas. The opening questions were all about Jewish education, and a rather lively debate soon sprang up about the pros and cons of day school versus supplementary school.

---

[2]Because we were short of time, we added it to the Shabbat program, placing it between Kiddush and lunch and replacing a different kind of study session that had been slotted in there.

[3]In my words, according to my "postgame analysis."

Then someone said something like, "I'd like to ask those of you with children who are counselors here this week what you think you did right as parents to have produced teenagers who are so positive about their Judaism and so involved, seemingly of their own free will?" The entire tone of the evening changed in the aftermath of her question. Thereafter almost all the questions were directed to the panel members who had children on the staff. Events took a dramatic turn when someone noticed that some of these offspring were in the room. (The counselors who were not on shmirah had dropped in on the adult Oneg Shabbat, perhaps out of curiosity but possibly for the refreshments or with a thought of throwing in a challenging question.) The counselors were asked if they would feel comfortable sharing their points of view. Three different young women spoke, focusing on the issues of finding their own way within a rather clearly structured Jewish environment.

While this was going on, a counselor seated beside me (whose father was not a rabbi) turned to me and whispered, "I think these parents are missing the point. What they need to know is that it is not because these fathers are *rabbis* but because these fathers are Jewish *role models*." I asked him if he would share his observation with the whole group. He said he was willing to do so. Returning to my role as moderator, I called on him and he repeated his observation to the room full of parents. He began with something about his own background—two nonrabbinic parents who were very devoted lay leaders in the Jewish community and who were divorced when he was young—and gave a humorous version of his expulsion from Jewish day school for wild behavior. He went on to say that it was the Jewish role modeling parents did for their kids that reflected the fact that Judaism was part of who they really were and not just something they did *for* their kids or required *of* their kids. The program ended with this sophisticated observation by a college junior. The atmosphere had been electrified, and intense conversations over coffee went on for a very long time.

Following up on that evening's turn of events, the staff decided to change the last night's program, planned as a mass team Pictionary competition, into an opportunity to delve into the area of concern that the Oneg Shabbat program had revealed. It became a program in which the counselors constituted a panel that the parents had a chance to question. (We removed the "rabbinic children" from the panel and put them all on shmirah.) Parents asked questions about everything from Kashrut to interdating. It was an intense and provocative evening, leaving everyone with much to think about as they headed home the next day.

One of the most telling conversations I ever had about this aspect of Family Camp took place the next morning when one of the parents said to me, "Vicky, I had a vision last night, and I use the word vision very carefully. My vision was that our new home which we are going to begin building has to have a kosher kitchen. I had this vision listening to the kids [on the panel] last night. You know,

I'm a physician. I read a lot of research, and sometimes you read all this stuff and suddenly something jumps out and you find yourself saying, Hey, maybe cancer and smoking *are* related! Well, that's how I felt listening to those kids . . . I felt like, Hey, maybe Kashrut and growing up to have a positive Jewish identity *are* related!"[4]

This is a fairly dramatic postscript to the main story, but it does make the point. This father had a sense of what he wanted for his three young sons (aged eighteen months, five and seven), and he listened carefully, drawing on what he heard for some kind of guidance.

The presence of these spirited, young adult Jews as role models helped parents gain courage and enthusiasm as they looked down the long parenting road that lay ahead.

Guidelines for Staffing

Naturally the total number and kinds of staff you can hire will be affected by considerations of budget, space and the numbers and ages of the participating children. The basic number you must establish at the beginning, the number you cannot cut, is the number of counselors. This is because the counselors provide the base on which the whole program rests. The safety and enjoyment of the children when they are in the children's program is one of the critical ingredients in the success of the program.

At minimum, in forty-eight-hour retreat settings you will need to fill these roles: director, kids' counselors, a music person, an adult teacher/facilitator and a tefilla leader. You might also wish to add, depending on site, season and local talent, a dance person, a lifeguard and an outdoor education person. It helps to look for someone with more than one talent. For example, your tefilla person might also be someone who can lead dancing. Budgetarily speaking, this is a good way to go because the range of activities you can offer is increased but your overhead is not (the person may do two jobs but only occupies one bed and eats one meal). If the additional responsibilities are not very demanding, you may not have to double the salary (although you will have to pay more).

---

[4] It is important to note two things here: (1) This is just one example of the impact of the counselor-models. Other parents probably felt similarly about an entirely different aspect of what was said during the panel or observed during the week. (2) Kashrut is not a topic that was part of the formal "curriculum" at camp. It is not something we teach about or teach to—it is just how we eat.

Director

The director needs to be someone who has four strengths: administration, Jewish knowledge, a feeling for the complexity of Jewish family life and a sense of fun. In addition, it helps to be flexible (able to adapt or change plans when circumstances require it), able to make many quick decisions and move on without agonizing, willing to be the "bad guy" (that is, the rule setter and enforcer for children—"No one may take the frogs out of the pond"—and for adults—"Can you please get Josh's shoes for him? He's barefoot and we're really trying to be consistent about the rule that everyone must wear shoes") and able to go without much sleep for the period of the encampment. Look for someone with a strong Jewish background and experience in nonformal or informal education, who is able to relate to adults, teenagers (staff) and children (in that order of importance). Ideally such a person will have had some experience with families, perhaps even some basic studies in family systems. It might work to create a team of two people who have complementary skills (an early childhood person and a camp director type; a Jewish Family Service staff person with family skills and a youth worker) who can collaborate together and share the limelight.

Counselors

Good counselors are the key to a successful retreat. First and foremost, it is only when parents feel their children are safe and having a good time that they are able to tune in and absorb the adult part of the program. Seeing *one* child wander by alone is sufficient for every parent to click off the discussion (no matter how fascinating) and become absorbed in concerns such as, Where is this kid headed alone? Where are the counselors? Where is my kid? Is anyone watching her? At that point the program, has, for all intents and purposes, ended.

Well-prepared and enthusiastic counselors help facilitate the smooth flow of all areas of the program. They help lead dancing by interspersing themselves along the circle. They lend their voices to singing sessions and tefilla. They help run the games at Family Fun Night, serving as team captains and game leaders. They supply extra laps for kids to sit on at group gatherings.

As noted above, counselors become the positive Jewish teen role models that parents of younger children need to see. Parents need to know that these kinds of teenagers exist and need the opportunity to interact with them. Parents are inspired to think that Jewish and parenting decisions they make now can have an impact on the kind of teenager their own children will turn out to be. This is very empowering. (To parents of a younger child, the teenage years often appear to be a dark land at whose borders they will totally lose custody of their child, who will become a mindless, oddly dressed automaton with a mind empty of all but "sex, drugs and rock and roll.")

How many counselors do you need? A basic rule of thumb is a starting number of at least two counselors for each age-group, plus one "floater." Even a small retreat (of about fifteen families) will almost always require that children be organized into three age-groups. (Of course, one of the challenges of a family retreat is that you never know the numbers or ages of children who will be enrolling until your registration is complete. In a series of retreats your groupings may be different every time.) But this is a rule of thumb to start with.

If you include two-year-olds in the children's program, you will need a ratio of one counselor to two children for that age group. For three-year olds, a ratio of one to three will work. For every group, it is important to have a minimum of two counselors so that if there is a problem (someone trips and needs a Band-Aid or ice; someone needs a parent), one counselor can attend to the problem and one counselor can be with the other children and keep the activity going.

What to look for in a counselor. As many of these characteristics as you can find in one teenage person: enthusiasm, positive Jewish identity, involvement in ongoing Jewish study and activity, self-confidence, ability to improvise, ability to think clearly and sensibly in a crisis, flexibility (ability to change plans to go with the flow), genuine liking for kids and comfort with physical (affectionate) contact, a sense of humor, ability to work well with peers, zest for the project, and ability to adapt quickly and catch on to a new situation fairly rapidly. Someone who takes too much time to make the transition to a new environment is a liability at such a short intense event. *Sechel* (common sense) is critical—IQ less so.

In general, look for a softer, warmer, sweeter teenager with a less "macho" style—someone (to the extent you can sense this) likely to be able to pay closer attention to the needs of the children and families and less to her own, someone who is comfortable enough with herself to be able to work with and under the scrutiny of adults.

You also need to ask yourself what kind of initial impression a particular counselor will make on adults. "Wholesome" wins out here. This is not to say that the ponytailed and earringed young man or the green-punk-haired young woman is to be automatically excluded. But carefully consider the implications of your choice and what it says to parents. Retreats, long and short, are very intense and require a fast start. The trust of parents and kids at initial meetings is critical. Warm-up time is often a nonexistent commodity. By the same token, time for training and supervision is at a premium—so the people you choose and train beforehand have to be ready to move out and function at full speed when you blow the whistle.

You probably will not find a whole staff that meets this profile, but go for it! You will find some who have many of these traits. Build staff around them, choosing others with complementary strengths and weaknesses. Trust your intuition—but also talk with others who are familiar with your candidate in various situations.

Where to find counselors. Start in your community's Jewish programs for teenagers—your local Hebrew high school, summer camp staff, and youth movements. If you are near a university, the Hillel on campus may be a good source of candidates. Ask around—some family's terrific babysitter, niece or nephew or next door neighbor may be just right. One of your top counselor candidates may have a best friend or a sibling who fills the bill.

It is a good idea for the director to make contact with the possible candidate directly, with an explanation of the program and an invitation to join the staff. It helps to say, "You've been recommended by ——." For a small selective program, this makes more sense (and fewer waves) than an ad or flyer. The contact can be made by telephone or by mail. (See p. 141 for a sample letter designed for recruiting new staff.)

Music Person/Song Leader

A good music person/song leader is indispensable to the structure of a successful retreat or camp experience, because music is one of the basic building blocks in the creation of both mood and community. (See the section on music and singing in chapter 7.)

What kind of person to look for. The ideal family retreat music person is someone who is a combination of good teacher and camp song leader. The good-teacher skills include giving clear instructions, making it easy and inviting to sing, exerting a firm guiding hand, managing the group and being able to "read" the group and move on, linger or change pace accordingly. The skills of a camp song leader include enthusiasm, spontaneity, the ability to read a group and an instinct for creating a group singing experience in which the spotlight shines on group energy and not on the song leader himself. A good teacher will often have the skills of a camp song leader, but the reverse is not always the case. (Look for someone who also plays the guitar.)

It is important to keep in mind that the person you choose needs to have tolerance for teaching or leading in a setting in which not everyone will be singing with undivided attention. (Someone may be nursing a baby, a toddler may be crawling around, two kids may be sitting on the edge playing with their shoelaces and so on.) As always, a sense of humor is a must.

Ideally, the person's repertoire should include the basic songs you want to sing—what you think might be common knowledge and what you would like to teach. If you find the right person but she does not know the songs, she can learn them in preparation for the retreat.

Where to look for your music person. If you do not have someone on your own staff, ask local camp directors and school directors. Check out your local youth movements. If you are near a university, look among students involved in Hillel or the Jewish students union—there may be a song leader among the students. A local school music teacher or chorus director may be the right person, requiring only some persuasion on your part and some orientation and training. An otherwise good choice—or your best available choice—can learn the songs you want to use from sheet music and tapes.

What if you cannot find a music person? Do not cancel the retreat! While it is true that music is the most potent mood creator and community builder, it is certainly not the only one! One or more of your counselors or other staff members who can carry a tune can certainly get the group going on basic common-knowledge songs—"la-la-la" songs, wordless songs and songs like "Hinay mah tov" and "Oseh Shalom." Use songs that the children have learned in pre-school or religious school as a good base for group singing. That way you start with a sizable group that is already familiar with the songs. Ease the introduction of a new song by teaching it to the staff beforehand (see staff meeting as described below, pp. 88 and 90). Keep new Hebrew songs simple and short. Select English-language songs with Jewish content for ease of singing and relevance to theme or calendar.

Remember—some singing is just of the "Take Me Out to the Ballgame" and "She'll Be Comin' 'Round the Mountain" variety. You might be able to split the singing between two staff people with complementary skills.

Another way to structure this role is to have one person who leads the whole group and someone else who works with small groups (the children when they are with their counselors, the adults learning a song for the good-bye circle and so on).

Tefilla Leader

The centrality and importance of this role is in direct proportion to the importance of prayer in your retreat and to the amount of time spent at prayer. If you are only having Kabbalat Shabbat, then you can probably get by without a specialist, whereas you cannot if you are going to have several services on Shabbat and weekday mornings. Its importance is also in indirect proportion to the degree of familiarity and comfort of your participants in the realm of prayer. If you will have a group that is not synagogue and prayer oriented, the role of the leader is much more central and much more difficult than with a more traditionally Jewish group.

What to look for. Someone who is knowledgeable about prayer, has a good voice and can command the attention of a large, mixed age-group. This has to be someone who can create a mood that helps people transition from other activities to prayer, using story, song, wordless melody or quiet. Like the music person, the tefilla leader on a family retreat has to be comfortable working without undivided attention. The leader needs to use words sparingly, providing a minimal number of brief and clear explanations and letting the experience wrap around people. (Answer questions later.) She needs to be able to maintain a finger on the pulse of the group, constantly monitoring the time and the pace, judging when to speed up and when and what to leave out or add before the group is lost. Clearly, for many settings this needs to be someone who will be comfortable if educational concerns shape halakhic requirements. Successful styles of tefilla leading run the gamut from the entertainer or cheerleader type who creates an upbeat kind of tefilla, to someone with a quieter, "warm and fuzzy" style. Both work.

Where to look for a tefilla leader. Check your own staff—could your rabbi or cantor fit into this kind of format? You might have a teacher on your staff who could manage this. A teenager might have the knowledge and the enthusiasm, but it is rare that teenagers have the necessary group skills and presence. Can your music person handle this? Or can you combine two staff members who complement each other and who can colead the tefilla?

Adult Teacher/Group Facilitator

This slot might be filled by one person or by two people who have slightly different expertise. The "teacher" is a scholar-in-residence type responsible for the teaching of Jewish content. The "facilitator" will take responsibility for the "family stuff" discussions. In some arrangements these two foci for adult learning can be structured to overlap. How you set this up will depend completely on what kind of study experience you want to create and whom you choose to do each piece.

What to look for. Seek someone who is an interesting teacher. Lecture style and inquiry style can both be successful in grabbing and maintaining learners' interest, but I lean toward the inquiry approach because I think it begins to detach participants from the more usual "life-support system" in which an expert *gives* them Jewish knowledge. Inquiry and discussion begin to give participants some responsibility for their own learning. The teacher should be someone with insight into and compassion for family life, because this important aspect of learners' lives will surface in class discussion. Choose someone who will enjoy spending time with the participants, at meals and on the ball field as well as in class.

Honoraria

The scale you set for honoraria will depend upon the particular job description, the length of the retreat and the "going rate" in your community. Here are some guidelines from various programs which were all working within constraints of a break-even budget. This may be dated by the time you read it or it may not apply to your community. Check with a local camp or youth director to ascertain the going rate.

- Counselors: for a weekend—$25 for an eighth grader (who was a "helper"), $50 for high school students and $75 for university students; for a five- or six-day camp—$100 for eleventh grade junior counselors, $125 for twelfth graders and $150 for all counselors older than that.

- Music person: from $250 for a weekend retreat to between $500 and $750 for a five- or six-day camp.

- Tefilla leader: this would depend a lot on who the person is, how much preparation is involved and how much tefilla there will be. Use your music person and adult teacher honoraria as a guide.

- Adult teacher/scholar-in-residence: $250 for a weekend with about three one-and-a-half-hour sessions to $500 for a longer camp with about nine hours of teaching.

Staff Training

Before a Forty-Eight-Hour Retreat

For a forty-eight-hour retreat that is held during the school year, the time you have available for training is minimal. (This is the reason why some of the characteristics mentioned above are so important. The counselor has to be able to "get it" with a minimum of direction and run with the ball. You have to trust that she will be able to do so.) You probably have time for one staff meeting.

Your best bet will probably be a Sunday evening about two weeks before your weekend. Plan the meeting to run from four o'clock in the afternoon through seven or eight o'clock at night, and plan to serve supper (pizza is usually a good choice) about halfway through. Include counselors, your music person and any other staff you think would be helped by preparing together. (You will need additional time to meet with your specialists such as the music person, but often this is easier to schedule as it will be one-on-one.)

Staff Meeting Outline

1. Introductions

2. Outline of the project: definition of family education—why we are involved in it and why it is important; how family camping is different from other kinds of camping they may be familiar with;

where each staff member fits in; counselors' importance to the success of the weekend

3. Describe the site (if it is unfamiliar to staff), stressing assets and problems; include any unique rules or dangers. (For example, at a site with a pond or lake: staff may not take kids out in rowboats. This is *only* a child-parent activity. If you want to go out in your free time, you may do so *only* if wearing a life jacket.)

4. Go over the schedule, highlighting staff members' responsibilities at different times. Special attention needs to be spent on differentiating between those times counselors are directly responsible for kids alone (usually when there is a planned activity for parents)—for which they need to program—and times they need to help facilitate a large group activity. Go over the shmira system and schedule (as well as the kitchen schedule if staff members have responsibilities in that area).

5. If there is a theme for the retreat, describe what it is and how it will play out over the weekend—what activities have been planned or are suggested that relate to the theme? What role will music play in relation to the theme? If there are specific songs relating to the theme that the songleader will introduce, this meeting is a good time for other staff to learn or review these songs.

6. Give out lists of kids by age-group and group assignments for staff; share any specific information you have about individual kids and families that might be important to know in advance.

7. Supper

8. Break into small planning meetings consisting of those who will be working together. First they need to plan several age-appropriate name games and mixer games for their group to play at their initial meeting. After that they need to come up with "lesson plans" for the other blocks of time they are responsible for planning. It is helpful to "prime the pump" with a hand-out listing games that children of the different ages enjoy playing. Include indoor and outdoor choices consistent with the weather possibilities and the kind of spaces your site offers. (See the sample games memo on p. 201.) Have resources available such as storybooks, crafts instructions, books of games and outdoor activities. As counselors meet in their subgroups, move from group to group, helping with ideas and making sure that the decisions are age-appropriate.

9. Have groups come back together and share their plans in outline form. Compile a list of required sports equipment and art supplies.

10. Give some helpful hints: the importance of being at the meeting place (where group time starts and groups assemble

with their counselors) five minutes before group time starts, so that kids and parents feel the counselors' readiness and the hand-off from parent to counselor goes more smoothly; the need to be ready with circle games to start with even before everyone gets there, so children (and parents) feel as if the program is getting going.

11. Be sure to cover what to do if there is a problem—a kid gets hurt, a kid has trouble separating and so on.

12. Answer questions that counselors may have.

13. Close with a reminder of how important the family experience will be for families' Jewish and family lives and how important the staff is in creating the experience. Make sure all staff members have rides to the campsite and that they know what to bring with them (sleeping bags, flashlights, tallit and *tefillin** and so on).

Before a Five- or Six-Day Camp

Try to arrange for a 24-hour staff orientation period prior to the arrival of the families. It is desirable to allot more time for training not just because there is more to be planned than for a forty-eight-hour retreat but because the collaborative component of the staff's work is even more important. Such a long encampment is intense, and things tend to move fast. Much of the success will depend on the ability of staff to work together to make decisions and share insights and responsibilities.

An example of scheduling for this kind of training period: If families will be arriving by lunchtime, ask counselors to arrive during the afternoon of the previous day. Have an afternoon session devoted to helping staff members get to know each other and to team building. After dinner together, use about an hour and a half or two hours for a more serious theoretical/educational meeting, after which people can break up into their small groups for planning and preparation. The next morning after tefilla and breakfast, there should be time allotted for finishing up on preparation and planning. Then, on a rotation basis, staff should be available to help families unload and move in.

The meeting agenda might be very similar to the outline for a shorter retreat (p. 87) but there is more time for orientation and theory before the staff needs to get into the nitty-gritty details of the program.

Agenda for Staff Meeting

1. Getting to know you:
   - Each staff person introduces herself and tells why she is here.
   - Play a few "name games": include one or two old standby games and a few brand-new ones; this will serve to warm

counselors up and give some models for their own first meeting with their campers.

- Form groups of three or four and play One-Minute Autobiography. Allow a few minutes of silence for thinking, after which each group member in turn can deliver a one-minute autobiography.

    Or play Live Wires: each group member gets a length of wire or long pipe cleaner. The assignment is to use the wire to make something that tells or represents something important about yourself. Individuals can then share their wire creations in small groups or in the large group.
- This is a great time to do some group singing—old favorites and any songs that may not be known by everyone, along with any new songs that will be taught during camp.

2. Theory/education. This part can be a guided discussion in which some of your educational theory, your goals for the week and the unique aspects of working with the whole family begin to come together for your staff. (See below for three options for this part of the meeting.) Whichever approach you choose for this meeting, be sure to close with a summary and link the theoretical conversation to the work of the week coming up.

3. Important details. Be sure to cover the following:
   - Some of the issues involved in being a counselor "under the eyes" of the parents, issues of shared responsibility for the health and safety of the children, what to do if a parent comes to the counselor with a problem or if the counselor perceives a problem with a parent.
   - The structure of the camp for the week—lines for communication and responsibility
   - The schedule
   - Particular health and safety rules (such as no bare feet outside, what to do for a bee sting and so on).

4. Singing. Review old favorites, teach any important new songs.

5. Work groups. After the whole group meets, staff should divide into small groups for work and preparation. Teachers (all together and then perhaps divided into those teaching kids and those teaching adults) can meet together to share ideas and lesson plans. Counselors should meet by age-groups to make their kids' nametags and group banner for orientation and to begin planning their week's activities.

    Spend some time at each group's meeting to answer any questions that have developed, help with ideas and suggestions, monitor progress and get a sense of the working climate of the group.

6. Snack. Be sure to provide an evening snack and some informal socializing time.

Three Options for Theory/Education Discussion
Camp and Families

1. Ask staff members to find partners—someone they do not know or someone they have not spoken to in a year. Tell them to take two or three minutes to talk and find how many things they have in common.

    Process this with them: How did it go? Was this hard or easy? Were similarities deep or superficial? Did camp come up? Did family things come up?

2. Ask each person to introduce his partner to the group.

3. Ask each pair to find another pair and form a foursome (preferably a combination of returning staff member and new staff member).

4. Give each small group of four a piece of paper and a pen. Ask them to fold the paper in quarters or thirds.

    Ask each group to list four good things about families. Ask each group to list four good things about camp. Ask each group to list potential good things that they can imagine happening in a camp for families.

    Bring all the foursomes back into one large group to hear and discuss what the different small groups have written. Come to consensus, if possible, on what is most important.

5. Discuss what you would like to send your families home with from this family camp experience.

    A less-structured variation: What do you know about camp? (What is good about camp when it works?) What do you know about families? (What is good about families when they work?) What do you think we might get if we combine them? That is, what does camp have to offer families?

Metaphors for Family

1. Begin with some "warm-ups":
    - Think of someone you know; compare that person with a tree or flower; share aloud the comparison (you do not need to reveal who the person was).
    - Think of a favorite Biblical character; what animal would you compare that person with?
    - You are the ocean. How do you look? How do you feel? What is it like to be the ocean?
    - What household appliance would you say that school is most like?
2. Explain something about metaphors and how they enrich our ideas by widening our definitions of things: "It's raining cats and dogs," "She is a real wet blanket," "He came into the room like a tornado."

People have used metaphors to describe the family as well. Two very famous metaphors are encapsulated in book titles about the family: *The Family Kaleidoscope* and *The Family Crucible*. Talk a little bit about crucibles and kaleidoscopes. As a large group, examine these questions: How is a family like a kaleidoscope? How is a family like a crucible? List as many answers as you can come up with. What do these two metaphors have in common? Important factors that should emerge from the discussion: each part is affected by the proximity of the other parts; the movement of each part affects the other parts; the whole is greater than the sum of its parts; every individual component and all the components' relationships with one another are affected by factors impinging from outside; each part retains its individual role yet mingles with the others.

Can the group come to consensus on which is a better metaphor for family? (When I did this with a group of staff, I discovered that we had to talk first about a definition for crucible. In fact it turns out that the meaning of the metaphor is that the family is both the crucible and, simultaneously, its contents.)

3. Have small groups work to brainstorm a list of as many original metaphors for family as they can. They should then explore each metaphor on their list and see if their small group can come to consensus about the most expressive single metaphor.

4. Listen to the small group choices and the reasons for those choices. (Some of the metaphors my group came up with: the family is like a salad, an ice-cream sundae, a fruit salad, a roller coaster, a stew, a mobile . . .)

5. Summarize what has come to light about families: what they are like, what makes them tick—and what difference that makes if we are going to create a learning environment for families.

Building an Educational Environment

1. Pose this question: One way of thinking about family camp is to imagine a family arriving here at our camp as an X; our job is to send the family home as $X+1$. If you could guarantee you would send them home with something, what would your choice for the $+1$ be?

2. Allow thinking time and then have each person write their choice for $+1$ on a small slip of paper or an index card. Read all the choices aloud and assemble a composite list.

3. Consider and discuss all the choices. Do these fall into categories? Which do you think we can do? Are there any that are more important than others?

4. How can we organize ourselves and our resources to accomplish what we want to?

9 Evaluation

EVALUATION is a vast and complex specialty within the discipline of education. In this section I will deal with a very tiny segment of this specialty—the role of evaluation in the kind of project dealt with by this book.

The first step in the evaluation process is taken at your first planning meeting when you ask yourself (and whatever group you are doing the planning with) the question, What will success look like? How will we know we have succeeded? How will our camper families be changed because they participated in our family camp? (For example, minutes of the initial meeting of the planning group that worked on the first Ramah Family Camp include the following: "We will know we have succeeded if families form havurot and continue to study and celebrate together after camp.")

The second step is taken when you ask yourself, How will we find this out? Will this be something we will be able to observe during the retreat? Will this be something we will find out from a questionnaire on the last day? Will this be something we will find out from a discussion at a reunion a month later? A questionnaire six months later? By asking returnees at our next retreat?

Evaluation lets you know how participants judge their experiences at the moment when they are going through the evaluation process. A questionnaire is the simplest and most effective way to get lots of immediate and structured feedback.[1] A questionnaire provides a kind of snapshot of how someone is feeling at the moment of filling out the questionnaire. This can be thought of as a kind of consumer-satisfaction survey, which will tell you whether people liked the program or not and what they did and did not like. If you plan to use the feedback from your participants to improve and fine-tune your program for next time (always keeping in mind that "next time" will probably have a different population, which in turn will have a different set of needs, expectations and group chemistry), decide what information you need and then what to ask in order to find that out. Often the information will fall into several categories: food, site and

---

[1] The hand-outs section contains four different evaluation questionnaires (pp. 205ff.).

facilities, staff, program, overall impressions, suggestions for improvement and intention/desire to return.

Collecting Feedback

The best time and place to collect feedback is while you have a "captive audience"—when everyone is still at the retreat. Set aside a time in the program when the whole group can sit down, preferably at tables (in a room with locked doors!), and have space and quiet to do a thoughtful job. This should take place as close to the end of the retreat as possible. When we first scheduled an evaluation session at Ramah Family Camp, we wrote it into the schedule *and* we prepared a hand-out, which we put in everyone's box. This explained the importance of evaluation in a serious education endeavor and why we needed everyone's input. (For an example, see p. 204.) I think that this helped people to see the evaluation session as an integral part of our educational work (and not just potential packing-up time). I also think that participants were persuaded that their reactions and comments would be important to the future of the Family Camp project.

At Shabbat Camp we rarely specify evaluation in the program. We just add the evaluation session at the beginning or the end of the Sunday morning "family stuff" session, because almost everyone is there and it is as close to the close of the retreat as we can gather everyone together. At Shabbat Camp we often use a few minutes of this time to explain something about the history and funding of Shabbat Camp, putting in a "plug" for the Agency for Jewish Education and the Federation. Then we explain the purpose of the evaluation process and give out questionnaires to be completed before we begin the "family stuff" session.

If you give out a questionnaire with a request for people to "do it when you have time and hand it in before you leave," many of the questionnaires will be lost, packed, dropped in the pool or made into paper airplanes. If you give it to people to take home and mail in, you will get even fewer back and you will miss the snapshot component of how people were feeling while they were still "in it." If you mail one to people later on, you will also get fewer than you need, and participants' reactions will already be cooler and more distant. (This can be very helpful too, but it is best as a complement to your initial questionnaire.)

If you have the staff time (personnel and budget) to do a follow-up, I suggest a follow-up phone call interview by someone who was at camp. Such an interview can contain as few as three or four questions that can be briefly answered but will help you build a more long-range picture of the retreat's impact.

Assessing Data

Keep in mind the idea of the snapshot. When you have a set of completed evaluation questionnaires, what you have is a collection of snapshots, one of each adult on the retreat. Their responses will be as varied as they are. Open-ended questions will accentuate this variety, although they will often elicit the most colorful and helpful answers. A multiple-choice questionnaire—which uses a number scale ("on a scale of one to five, five being highest . . .") or the choice of "yes/no" or "always/sometimes/never"—will provide more easily comparable questions but less detail. I have often found it useful to include both types of questions. (After the first Ramah Family Camp, an evaluation discussion held by the staff included the following comment: "100 percent of our families said they would like to return next summer. Is this success?" The consensus of the group: "Yes and no." It felt good to know that people had had such a good time that they felt it was worth organizing their summer and their vacation finances in order to come back. But it was not quite enough for our group, which had established a set of more transformative goals for the experience. Fortunately, the evaluation questionnaire that we had participants complete on the last morning asked many more questions, so we did have more data to go on.

Some examples of the complexities of assessing the whole snapshot album: The first-year evaluations of Ramah Family Camp featured many comments about the amount of junk food available, particularly the chocolate chip cookies for which the baker was well known. In the next year we worked hard to eliminate the sugar snacks and replace them with healthier choices. The evaluations that second year were split between those who said, "Thank you for the carrots and celery snacks," and those who longed for the return of the luscious chocolate chip cookies they had kept in mind all winter. Snapshots. Food at one Shabbat Camp was described as "perfect," "too starchy," and "too healthy." Snapshots. The same program may be described by different participants as "too structured" and as having "too much free time." Snapshots. This kind of wide divergence will usually tell you more about individual participants than about your program. You and your staff need to sift and balance and make decisions from the vantage point of your best judgment. Look for the points of consensus.

Always ask participants for suggestions for improving the program. We have gotten some excellent help from the suggestions of people who have enjoyed the program, have taken it seriously and would like to return. The most difficult aspect for the program director is that suggestions for improvement imply lack of perfection, which can feel personal for some of us. Try to take suggestions as honest help offered toward making a meaningful experience even better.

Role of evaluation for the participants. Certain kinds of questions can help them reflect on their experience and its potential impact on their lives. This is a critical component of the kind of intense experience that retreats provide. I will often include sentence completions covering topics such as these: "A personal highlight moment for me was . . ."; "A personal highlight moment for my family was . . ."; "I think our next Jewish step will be . . . ." Do not let people go home without an opportunity to put some thoughtful closure on the experience."The answers to the participants' reflections on their experience also provide important feedback for the program team. What *were* the most meaningful moments for people? What *are* people taking home with them? What do they suspect will make a *difference* in their lives? These are the critical features that make a retreat worth all the energy that goes into it. If you do not know the answers to these questions, you do not know anything.

If you have returnees to your program, you have a golden opportunity to find out what difference their previous participation made in their lives. This is the kind of data we need when we make our case for the importance of doing a retreat to our boards, our funding sources and ourselves.

Public relations and recruitment tool. Do you need to persuade a board that the participants found the experience worthwhile? Do you need to make a case for funding or scholarships or a change in your institutional calendar? Do you need some blurbs from real live happy campers for your next brochure? The kind of evaluation you do can provide you with these as well.

Long-term assessment. To assess the long-term impact of the program on people's lives, you would need initial responses and a series of follow-up reflections over the months and year. This is a more extensive (and expensive) kind of research, and to date the funding sources in the Jewish community have not been interested in this kind of longitudinal study.

Evaluation of the retreat by the staff. This is also a critical phase in any on-going, serious educational endeavor. At any retreat or family camp, I have always tried to make time for three kinds of staff evaluation: In the middle—how are things going? Do you see any problems? Suggestions? At the end—initial reactions, comments, suggestions, criticisms. A month later—a meeting for more thoughtful consideration of issues that emerged during the retreat, in participants' questionnaires, and from the staff.

10 Lesson Plans

Raise Your Hand If—A Parents' Getting-to-Know-You, Warm-up Activity

Perfect while waiting for people to get together. Easily adaptable for kids.

"Raise your hand if..."

- You were born and raised in (California)
- You have spent time in Israel
- You ever went to camp as a child
- You remember your nursery school teacher
- You have ever made hallah from scratch
- You wore a costume this past Purim/you were at a seder of at least ten people (depending upon what the most recent holiday was)
- Your favorite flavor ice cream is chocolate/vanilla/other
- You are an A's fan/a Giants fan
- You do not care about baseball
- You are an "only child"/one of two children/one of three
- You are an oldest child/a youngest child/a middle child
- You have one child/two/three/more
- This is your first time here/your second
- You have had it with Ninja Turtles (or something else timely and trendy)

Pause between topics for people to look around, laugh and think.

As this activity gets rolling, participants should get the hang of it and join in with topics of their own. This generally adds to the laughter and begins to forge a spirit of fun for the group. This is also a way of learning something about your participants. Topics suggested by participants in groups I have started this way have included everything from Jewish education ("Raise your hand if you went to Hebrew school/day school/your kids attend/you belong to a synagogue") to demography ("Raise your hand if one of your siblings has intermarried/if you are a Jew by choice") to more personal issues ("Raise your hand if you have had a vasectomy").

Paper Bags—A First-Night Program for Parents

This activity helps people get to know one another in a very nonthreatening way and covers a mix of topics (Jewish and general) that are light and require no special knowledge. It also gets people talking and thinking (in the last round) about why they came to a Jewish family retreat, their motivations, their Jewish family stories.

Supplies: Paper lunch bags (one for each four participants plus a few extras) containing six to eight talk topics, each on a slip of paper (see below)

Space: Flexible—so people can move around, form groups, sit comfortably

1. Ask people to get up and find someone they do not know and have a two-minute conversation.

2. Ask them to take their partner, find another pair and introduce their partner to the two new people.

3. Ask everyone to sit down, get comfortable and decide who will be number one, two, three and four.

    Here I always give an overview of what is about to happen, without telling the topics. It is always important to reassure people that there are no embarrassing topics in the bag and that if they pull one that they absolutely cannot talk about, they can put it back and choose again. (This is also a reason to have more strips in the bag than there are people in the group.)

4. Give each group a brown bag. In the bag should be at least six slips of paper, each with a topic for discussion. (Although a group of four will actually only need four topics, putting six strips or even eight in each bag makes it easier for a group that may end up with five or six members.)

    The rules are these: At the signal, person number one pulls a slip, reads the topic or question out loud and then has two minutes to talk about the topic. Other participants cannot speak except to draw this person out *about this topic*. Then, at the signal, number two pulls a slip of paper and proceeds with that topic, and so on around the circle. If you have some groups with five or six members, get them to move on to their next speaker a little before you give the signal to the whole group.

    When all four people in each group have finished, give a few minutes for them to go back and talk about whatever unfinished business remains from their four topics; they can also choose to dip into the bag and talk about the remaining topics in a less structured way. (This last phase also yields time for the bigger groups to finish.)

5. Ask the groups of four to find another four and form groups of eight. Pose a question that goes something like this: What is it that brought you here with your family this weekend? There are many options for where to spend a holiday weekend—why is this the choice you and your family made?

   Judge from the intensity of the conversations as you monitor the room, but you should usually allow this part to go about ten to twenty minutes.

6. Wrap it up by saying something like, "I know it seems like we're just getting warmed up, but I do want to bring the structured part of the evening to a close so those of us who need sleep can get it. Please continue to talk—just remember that the counselors need their sleep too, and so you need to relieve them by —— P.M. We've just begun to get to know one another. It seems that most of us are just getting into this last question. Luckily, we have the whole weekend to continue to talk and explore and share ideas about families and parenting and being Jewish. I hope you'll use your time here to do that!"

Preparation

Choose eight topics. It works well to strike a balance between Jewish and general topics. Type these out, one underneath the other, on a sheet of paper. Make as many copies as you will need. Cut into strips. Put a different combination of six or seven in each bag.

Suggested Topics

- Talk about your favorite Jewish holiday.
- What part of the Sunday paper do you read first and why?
- What is the most beautiful place you have ever been?
- Describe your most treasured Jewish possession.
- If you could return to one year in your life, what year would it be and why?
- Describe your ideal synagogue.
- What is the most significant thing you did in the past week?
- If you could master a new skill, what would it be?
- Talk about someone who had an impact on your life.
- What is something you would like to see?
- If you could add any three people (living, dead, fictional) to your seder, who would be your choices and why?
- Share a favorite childhood memory.
- Seasonal questions: For example, as Rosh HaShana approaches, what is a hope you have for the new year? As Passover approaches, what is something you would like to be free of or help to free?

   The scaffolding here consists of choosing topics that are not too personal for most adults meeting strangers for the first time and that are a mixture of Jewish and general themes. The Jewish topics are selected to reflect a kind of generic Jewish knowledge. The Jewish and family themes are there to let participants know that Jewish issues are part of this family camp experience and part of what is important to know about each other.

Individual Incorporations—
A First-Night Mixer for Parents

1. "Find someone who . . . and introduce yourself." (You can use one or more of these categories.)

   - Has the same number of siblings as you do
   - Was born on the same side of the Mississippi as you were
   - Had the same favorite subject in school as you did
   - Had the same least favorite subject in school as you did

2. If you are a righty, find all the other righties. If you are a lefty, find all the other lefties. When you have found them, form one circle in alphabetical order by first names. Merge the smaller circles into one large circle in alphabetical order by first names.

3. Break into groups of five. Sit down and get comfortable.

   - Share a Passover memory (or something else seasonal that you can expect most people have had exposure to).
   - See how many answers you can come up with to this question: How is being a family like being on an airplane ride?

4. Form tens. Talk about what attracted you to this weekend; why are you here?

Four-Cornered Nametags—A First-Night Getting-to-Know-You Program for Parents

Supplies: 8½"×11" (or 8½"×17") paper, dark-colored markers or crayons.

1. Ask participants to hold the paper horizontally and print their name in the middle in large (two-inch) letters.

   - In the upper right-hand corner, write the name of a food you like so much you could live on it for a few days.
   - In the lower right-hand corner, write the initials of someone who influenced your life.
   - In the lower left, answer this question: If you had not chosen to be here with your family, where else in the world would be your second choice for a weekend (or week) away with your family?
   - In the upper left, write something you have learned from your children.

   Other possible topics:

   - The favorite lunch you pack for your kids for school
   - Write Yes or No: television is dangerous to children's minds
   - Write Yes or No: Hanukkah has gotten too commercial
   - The best book you have read with your kids
   - The best book you have read for yourself

2. Ask participants to stand up and, holding their nametags in front of them, mill around reading what other people have written without speaking to each other. After a minute or so for silent milling, ask them to nonverbally form groups of four, sit down and get comfortable. Direct groups to decide who will be number one, two, three and four within the group.

3. The activity proceeds this way: Each round of talking will focus on one corner of the nametag. Participant number one has a minute (or two) to talk about the first corner. During his speaking time, others have to listen and can speak only to ask the focus person questions that draw him out. Person number two takes a turn on the same topic, with the same rules, as talking time rotates around the group. Then all move on to the next corner as a topic of discussion. The second round can begin with person number two going first. And so on.

   You will need to be the time monitor with a bell or something similar to keep the talk moving. Ring to mark each turn and to get a new round (with a new corner topic) started. You may only have time to talk about three of the four corners, which is fine. Choose the three you think will work best or are most important, but always begin with the corner that is most neutral or fun (it provides a better warm-up).

If groups of more than four form, you can either remind them after a minute and a half to go ahead, ignore the bell or whistle and keep moving; or you can add two minutes of time after the completion of the corners for people in groups of four to ask questions and inquire about things that may have surfaced and participants want to return to while larger groups finish up.

4. I like to close with some sort of "whip" in which a sentence stub is posed for the whole group and we just go around with each participant finishing it in a personal way. A good choice: "Something I have learned from being a family member is . . . ." (This is enlightening and can also be very humorous.)

Gefilte Fish—A Program for Parents

A program using *Gefilte Fish*, the videotape.[1] An ideal evening program for parents, which can also be used as a daytime discussion.

Supplies: the videotape, a VCR and TV

1. Whip:
   - Tell something that was passed on to you.
   - Tell something you intend to pass on.

2. Unstructured comment, reaction, conversation: Common threads and differences in what people said in the "whips."

3. Did people mention tangible or intangible "inheritances" first time around? Do a second set of whips in which people mention something in the category opposite to that of the inheritances mentioned before.

   (When I first did this, I assumed that the participants' initial response to the whips in Step 1 would be to mention tangible items and that my role would be to discuss the various tangibles and then point out the fact that we also receive and hand on intangibles. However, by and large, people mentioned intangibles immediately in the initial whips. I did not need to introduce it. It was right there; I only had to point it out. I pointed out that everyone had mentioned primarily intangibles and that there were also tangibles. At that point, some people also talked about some of their thoughts about those tangibles. This was done in a conversation that was much less structured than the whips.)

4. View the video.

5. Unstructured initial response to video.

   (People plunged right in without any prompting from me, but if this had not happened, I would have begun with a question such as, What do you think? What was this about? Did anything in this video seem familiar to you?)

6. Miscellaneous discussion questions:
   - Is the amount of work involved in passing something on a factor in whether it is passed on?

     (Here we talked a lot about all the senses involved in making gefilte fish. Many participants felt strongly that it is not the making of the gefilte fish that is important but the celebration or ritual meal at which it is served—even if it is

---

[1] A fifteen-minute home movie–type video that presents three generations of women from one family and their different approaches to the art of gefilte fish. The video is available for $25.95 from Ergo Media, 668 Front Street, P.O. Box 2037, Teaneck, NJ 07666. Many Jewish community libraries and Jewish teacher resource centers have a copy of this for rental or borrowing.

from a jar. We also talked about special celebratory foods that are traditional in our families.)
- What is this video saying about the passing on of tradition?
- Which of these three generations are you closest to? Why?
- What is your prognosis for the youngest generation shown in this video?
- Is this only about mothers, that is, does it also apply to fathers? How?
- What if your parent or grandparent did not pass something on to you? What other choices do you have? What can you do about it?

(I tried to bring out the fact that the "passing on" is not always and not necessarily only from mother or grandmother to daughter—that those are not the only routes and that you are not "off the hook" because something was not passed on to you. If our grandmothers and mothers did not teach us something—but we want to do it or pass it on—we can still learn what we want to learn by finding a teacher. We thereby make ourselves into the first of a new chain. Many people shared examples of things they had learned: for example, learning to make hallah with their child in preschool or learning to make honey cake from a friend or learning to make *matzah** balls from the box label. I also pushed them to give other examples—from outside the culinary field— of Jewish skills and ideas they had learned.)

7. Closure: The video and discussion have asked us to think about what we want to pass on to our kids. It is a light movie that provides a framework for thinking about the role of parents.

   What did you do *today* to pass something that is important to you on to your kids? (Quiet time to think back over the day, followed by sharing of various things they had done.)

   Ask yourself that question daily.

8. People who want to then have an opportunity to view the video again.

"Family Stuff" 1: Sentence Stubs—A Family-Issues Program for Parents

This works equally well as an evening program or as a daytime program.

Supplies: Pencils for everyone, a hand-out for everyone (p. 179)

Space: Flexible, movable seating on chairs, benches or floor

This program is designed to get parents talking with one another about family issues. It is *not* a good first-night program, because its power is in direct proportion to the degree to which people feel comfortable enough to bring up their really burning issues. If the other elements of the program are successful and have built toward trust and openness and community, this kind of program can be slotted in after twenty-four hours. We have run it as a second-night program in a one-week camp and as a Sunday morning program in a weekend retreat. It is a good activity to use in an ongoing program such as a family havurah.

1. Sentence Stubs begins with some quiet time, during which each participant finishes the sentence stubs on the hand-out for herself. This should be done privately and not in consultation with anyone else. A helpful ground rule (if people ask, and sometimes they do) is that spouses should each fill a sheet out separately.

2. After people have filled these out, ask them to form groups of six to eight, depending on the size of your group and how long you have for the program, with spouses in separate groups. When everyone is comfortable, describe the framework for the discussions: Each person will have two (or three) minutes in which to talk about *one* of her sentences—whichever one she most wants to talk about or get help with. As the groups talk, spend a few minutes sitting with each group so that you get the pulse of the group, learn something about the families and also help a group out if it gets stuck.

3. You monitor the time, ringing a bell approximately every two minutes so that focus shifts and everyone has time to talk. When talk has gone around the circles, let people know that they now have time to ask each other questions, go back to topics left unfinished or bring up new topics that the group seemed interested in. After about fifteen minutes or so (you be the judge as you wander and monitor the pace and intensity of the different groups), call the group back together.

4. Close the evening by stating how hard it is to raise a family, how much harder it is to maintain a Jewish family, how good it feels to share these struggles with other parents and how good it feels just to know that other people have stood or stand in our place

and can help us out. You can use examples based on what you heard as you floated. You can summarize this by saying that the kind of sharing and support which characterizes this kind of family camp experience is what we hope people will carry home with them in the form of friendships and phone numbers.

5. Finish with one of two readings, depending on what you have emphasized in your wrap-up: "The Generations" (p. 185), which stresses the need for parents to make those Jewish decisions and participate in their children's Jewish life, or "Lost in the Forest" (p. 186), which stresses our role as parents in helping one another.

Preparation

Create your hand-out based on your selection from among these suggested[2] sentence stubs:

- Something our family loves to do together is . . .
- One of our happiest moments as a family was . . .
- A Jewish decision our family has made is . . .
- Some religious differences between my family now and the family I grew up in are . . .
- My current plans for my kids' Jewish education are . . .
- A Jewish wish I have for my family is . . .
- A Jewish parenting question I've always wanted to ask another family is . . .
- Something I'd like to tell my rabbi about the Jewish needs of my family is . . .
- The way we deal with the "December Dilemma" (Hanukkah/Christmas) is . . .
- My family needs . . .
- I'd like my family's next Jewish step to be . . .

Note: This activity is carefully scaffolded. It is designed to be safe for the participants. If everyone thoughtfully fills out the questionnaire, we will have helped people to reflect on family. The group sharing is structured so that people can choose to reveal as much or as little as they feel ready or comfortable doing. (The first and second sentence stubs are there because they are easy and not very personal, providing a kind of refuge for participants who are not comfortable sharing more.) Everyone benefits from listening to the conversation regardless of the level of personal participation. Remember, this activity structures the sharing of family concerns not as a limited event but as a portal to continuing conversations over dinner, by the ball field and over the telephone (back in the city).

---

[2]These all work. Make a selection (seven is a good number) that suits your population, or create your own based on what you know about your population and their issues.

"Family Stuff" 2:
Paragraphs—A Family-Issues Program for Parents

This program has the same purpose and the same caveats as Sentence Stubs. Do not use both in the same retreat, but the unused activity could be used in a second program that includes some of the same participants.

Supplies: Pencils for everyone; hand-outs for everyone (see below)

Space: Flexible seating

1. In this program, everyone gets a hand-out that includes a selection of paragraphs (between eight and ten) about family issues. Quiet time is set aside for reading through all the paragraphs. Ask participants to choose the paragraph they would most like to discuss with others. We ask them to write that paragraph number on the back of their pages and walk around holding the number in front of them, nonverbally forming groups of people who have made the same choice.

2. Ask people to settle down and talk about their chosen paragraph. Obviously, the groups will be of different sizes. The only problems caused by this are that one person is not a conversation (ask that person to make a second choice) and that more than seven or eight people in a group can be too cumbersome (divide eight into two groups of four).

3. After about twenty minutes (you be the judge as you monitor), ask people to make a second choice and repeat the process. (If a group does not feel that they are ready to move on, they can continue even as others regroup.)

4. Closure: Same as with Sentence Stubs

Preparation

Select eight to ten paragraphs. We include thirteen different paragraphs (pp. 181–183), which you can select from or use as a guide in choosing your own. It helps to have some knowledge of the issues that move your group. For a single-parent families' retreat, we included four paragraphs (of ten) dealing with divorce. For another group we made a different selection.

The paragraphs are selected to get people thinking and reflecting. Some of this happens just by reading the paragraphs, by being exposed to well-articulated, new or different ideas relating to family life. The paragraphs then serve as the context for conversation. I usually leave the citations off the paragraph sheets, because sometimes knowing the source can influence how something is read. (I give out a "footnote" (p. 184) sheet at the end of the activity.)

Family Incorporations—A First-Night Active Getting-to-Know-You Family Program

This is a good prelude to your first-night program.

1. "Find a family that . . . and introduce yourselves." (Choose one of these descriptions.)

   - Has the same number of members present as yours does
   - Has a different number of members present than yours does
   - Lives in your neighborhood
   - Has a kid whose birthday is in the same season as that of a kid in your family
   - Has a phone number ending with the same number that your phone number ends with
   - Has a member wearing the same color shirt as someone in your family
   - Has a member wearing the same kind of shoes as someone in your family is wearing

2. Play Ring-around-a-Rosy with the family you have found.

3. Up to this point, Family Incorporations can serve as a warm-up to your evening program. Go on to Family Banners (p. 110) or Family Pizza (p. 111).

   Or, if Erev Shabbat is the first night of your retreat, continue here with this Oneg Shabbat version:[3]

4. The Ring-around-a-Rosy circles can merge into one large circle for dancing *mayim* and *cherkassiyya* and then move into *tyish*.*

5. Go from *tyish* into kids' groups (by nametag symbols) for fifteen minutes of small-circle name games and other circle games while parents talk and play Raise Your Hand If . . .

6. Then go back to the circle for some quiet singing and a good-night song.

---

[3]See page 49 for an expanded description of this program.

Family Banners—A First-Night Program for Families

Supplies: Butcher paper cut into long rectangular strips or into "banner" shapes (one per family), baskets of markers or crayons to be passed around and shared.

Space: Large open space in which people can spread out and work as families on the floor or tables.

1. Ask each family to design a banner that tells the world important things about their family.
    Allow time for everyone to work. During this time, walk around and monitor families as they work. This will help you gauge the timing of this activity; more importantly, you will begin to learn about your families and about the various ways in which families work together. Counselors can circulate, helping people share crayons and so on.

2. Ask every family to take its finished banner, join up with another family or two, introduce themselves and explain their banners to each other.

3. Hang all the banners in the room you are using (if this is a room you will use other times). Otherwise hang them in some public place such as the dining room or the space you will be using as a synagogue.

Variation: Give each family a banner that is obviously designed and shaped to be held vertically. Ask them to write their family's last name (or names) one letter below the previous one along the left-hand margin. Ask them to choose a word describing their family to go along with each letter in their name, and then to decorate their banners.

Family Pizza—A First-Night Program for Families

Supplies: Large corrugated circles used under take-out pizza or under round cakes (available in various diameters from party supply places), baskets of markers to share

Space: Large open space in which people can spread out and work as families on the floor or at tables.

1. Talk a little bit about pizza—what different ingredients people like on their pizzas.

2. Ask them to imagine that their family is a pizza. What are the ingredients which make up their family pizza?

3. Distribute the pizza cardboards and markers, and ask them to illustrate their ideas about their family as a pizza.

4. Allow time for work.

5. Proceed as for Family Banners above (p. 110).

Drama Games—A Family Evening Program

1. Form groups of two to five families, using one of these methods:
   - Give a member of each family a colored tag or colored coding dot on the forehead or hand; they have to find another family (or families) with the same color.
   - Tell one member of each family a "secret" (consisting of a nursery rhyme title such as "Mary Had a Little Lamb" or "Twinkle Twinkle Little Star"). When every family has its secret, secret keepers can tell their families; then families walk around singing their secret and forming teams with others singing the same secret.

2. Ask groups to stand or sit in circles holding hands. Direct the following games: Pass the Squeeze, Cross Hands and Pass the Squeeze, Telephone, Duck-Duck-Goose.

3. Machines Charades: Hand each team an index card with an assignment written on it. Allow about five to ten minutes for preparation of their Machine Charade. Each team presents its machine, and other teams have to figure out what they are presenting.
   Suggested charades: vacuum cleaner, roller coaster, corn popper, pinball machine, ski lift, computer, clothes washer, boom box, tree, waterfall

4. Jewish Holiday Charades: Each team gets a three-by-five-inch card with the name of a Jewish holiday written on it, which they need to act out in mime for the others to guess.

5. The Nursery Rhyme Variety Show: Each team gets a three-by-five-inch card with its assignment printed on it. Suggestions: "Puff the Magic Dragon," "She'll Be Comin' 'Round the Mountain," "Frere Jacques," "London Bridges," "Mary Had a Little Lamb," "Jack and Jill," "Hey Diddle Diddle," "Sesame Street," "Pat-a-cake," "Take Me Out to the Ball Game." Groups have a few minutes to prepare a creative rendition of their nursery rhyme.

6. Spirals (in small groups): Everyone holds hands and steps back. Two people drop hands. One of those people stands still, not moving at all. The other begins to lead the line of people in walking around the outside of the circle and then spiraling around the stationary person, drawing everyone into a tighter and tighter coil until the group members are tightly wrapped around each other. Feel the group energy. Sing. Sway.
   Begin to unspiral: Do this from the center. Still holding hands, the person in the middle ducks down and begins to weave a way out of this forest of legs. Everyone has to follow. When

the group is uncoiled, it should find itself in a circle again, still holding hands.

7. Giant Lap Sit (a dynamite group-unity closing activity): This game ends up with your entire group in a circle and each person sitting on someone's lap.

    Ask each circle to break at one point (by dropping hands) and join hands with an adjoining circle. Once you have one large circle with everyone facing in, ask them to drop hands and step in closer so that they are almost shoulder to shoulder. Now ask people to turn so that right shoulders are all in toward the center of the circle and they are standing one behind the other. Ask everyone to place hands on the next person's waist. Then, making sure their own knees are together, everyone sits—each participant guided by the person in back of her onto that person's knees. (Actually, people end up more on knees than laps.)

8. Sing your Good-night Circle Song with everyone in lap-sitting position.

Family Fun Night—A Family Evening Program

This round-robin of games and challenges for the whole family is also called Solomon (Shlomo) Grundy. It usually involves earning points for each task accomplished, and it can be designed to be more competitive or less so. It is a great program for the end of Shabbat because it is very active and funny, thereby providing a good release from the quieter, more contemplative mood of Shabbat. Ideally it is played after Havdalah, but it can be a pre-Havdalah activity on a long summer Shabbat (depending upon the halakhic framework within which your program operates).

Help families form teams of families. The teams should be more or less the same size if possible, although the actual size of the teams is not critical. (A large team will not have a competitive advantage. Members of a small team will have more opportunities to participate but will not accumulate more points.)

The total number of teams has to be equal to or less than the number of stations. Usually the program starts with one team at each station. After a specified number of minutes of play, teams move on to the next station. There can be a team-less station (which is then occupied in the next round while another station will be empty—but it does not work as well if there is a team without a station.

The counselor assigned to each team is responsible for the score sheet and for fanning team spirit and getting everyone cheering for everyone else.

The score sheet can be just a piece of construction paper with the team name or number written across the top. When the team arrives at a station, the score sheet is handed to the counselor in charge of the station, who keeps track of the points earned. Do this with hatch marks as each point is accumulated, or use coding-dot stickers or reinforcements for each five points. (The stickers constitute an easy way to keep score if you are playing on Shabbat.)

Organization

Stations are set up around the perimeter of a large indoor room (a basketball or tennis court works too). Assign a staff member to each station and a staff member to each team. Setup is facilitated if the supplies for each station (and a large sign with the number of the station) are placed in a shopping bag and handed to the person in charge of each station. This can all be ready to roll before your retreat even begins. If you choose to slot this activity in on Saturday night, either before or after Havdalah, it can be set up in less than ten minutes.

It helps to give each team a few minutes to choose a team name. If you have a small group and only five or so teams, you can also have each team make up a cheer and present it to the group.

Send each team to a station and allow a minute for the station leader to demonstrate and explain the task. Blow a whistle (or use some other loud attention-getting noise) to let people know when to start. Allow three to five minutes for play (use your judgment and monitor how long the various games are taking); blow the whistle to signal that it is time to switch stations (be sure teams know in which direction to move); allow a minute for instruction and demonstration; blow the whistle to start play, and so on.

Additional Hints

- As you set up your space, arrange it so that teams will alternate more and less active games.
- Choose a selection of activities that work for most of your population—that is, keep your two-year-olds in mind, too.
- Do not use anything involving water.
- Do not use anything involving food—that type of game gives everyone a mixed message. (It is hard to teach about not wasting food and feeding the hungry if food is a prop for play.)
- Be creative . . .

Stations

Here are some time-tested, popular stations designed for simplicity of supplies.

Relays

The team keeps the activity going and gets a point for each person who completes the challenge.

- Large Ball Over-and-Under Relay
   Supplies: One basketball or foursquare ball

- Clothing Relay: Players line up; the first person dresses in assorted articles of clothing and dashes (or waddles) to a terminal point (go around a chair or tag the wall) and then back to the front of the line; as he undresses, the next person in line puts everything on and dashes off; the first person then runs to the back of the line.
   Supplies: Adult-size clothing such as extra-large boxer shorts, large bathrobe, size twelve or thirteen (or bigger) sneakers, a scarf or tie, a hat, mittens or gloves

- Balancing Relay: Walk to a terminal point and back with a Ping-Pong ball on a plastic spoon or a feather on a plastic spoon; adults can be asked to do this with a spoon in their mouth to make it more difficult.
   Supplies: A few plastic spoons, several Ping-Pong balls or feathers

- Skipping/Hopping Relay: Skip or hop or jump to a terminal point and back.

- Obstacle Course: A short course could involve walking around chairs, going under a bench, jumping over a line of rope or tape and back; older participants could be asked to skip through the course or do it going and coming back (with younger kids just doing it one way).

Supplies: Chairs, bench, line of tape

Group Collaboration

The counselor running this station has to be sure that adults and children alternate and that every team member gets a chance.

- Mr. Blockhead: Team builds a tower, trying to see how high they can go until the tower tumbles; they get a point for every block; when it tumbles they can try again.
  Supplies: This works best on a table around which the team can gather; you need two Mr. Blockhead games[4] or a selection of about twenty-five or thirty small blocks in a variety of shapes.

- Memory Board: Counselor has a tray on which a selection of objects is arranged and covered by a small towel or bandana. When everyone is ready, she removes the bandana and gives everyone a minute (or more) to study and memorize the objects. She then covers the tray again and team members take turns recalling the objects they have seen; they get a point for each one they remember. Counselor should have enough objects to do a few rounds of this.
  Supplies: This also works best on a table with the team gathered around it; tray and bandana; possible objects: toothbrush, comb, bar of soap, key, pencil, paper clip, *kippah*,[*] eraser, spoon, Hanukkah candle, Purim noisemaker, golf tee, penny, nail, scissor, mixing spoon, baseball schedule, balloon, mini-water gun, rubber band, barrette, mezuzah, Shabbat candle.

- Cup Tower: Similar to Mr. Blockhead but can be played on the floor; uses up those old (un-politically correct) Styrofoam cups; the object is to see how high a tower the team can build.
  Supplies: Paper or Styrofoam cups

- Name That Tune: If you have a piano in the room, use that; you can also use an accordion. Musician plays a song and the team has to guess and name the tune; they get a point for every tune named.
  Supplies: A musician and a suitable musical instrument

Tossing/Throwing Games

- Penny Toss: Team lines up; first person gets three pennies to pitch into a beach pail and then goes to the end of the line. Vary for age

---

[*]This is a commercial game.

by having a larger receptacle for younger kids to throw into or by having toe lines (in masking tape on the floor) at varying distances from the pail.

    Supplies: A roll of pennies, a beach pail (and a bigger bucket, if needed)

- Bowling: Team lines up and first person uses a tennis ball or foursquare ball (depending on the target) to knock over tall blocks, plastic bowling pins or plastic soda bottles weighted with sand.

    Supplies: Ball and three "targets"

Singdown—An Evening Program for Families

1. Form teams made up of several families. (An ideal team size has about eight to twelve members.) Each team gets paper and a pencil.

2. A topic is announced, and teams have a few minutes to list all the songs they can collectively think of that contain the key word or are on the general topic (depending on the rules established).

3. Play begins. Each team in turn sings one song from their list. Once a song is sung, it cannot be repeated. When a team runs out of songs or duplicates a song already sung, they are "out." The winner is the last team left with a song to sing on that round's topic.

   If the makeup of the group is tilted toward the younger ages, an alternative way of playing is to go a few rounds with one topic and then move on to a new topic. This keeps interest high and competition low; everyone wins.

Suggested topics

- Animals
- Sky (including things in the sky—clouds, stars, moon, sun)
- Ocean (including things in the ocean)
- Land (including things that grow from the land—grass, trees, flowers)
- Love
- Weather
- Shabbat
- Israel
- Holidays

Family Talk Collage—An Interactive Program for Parents and Kids Older than Six

This works as either a day or an evening program.

Supplies: One per family—colorful three- by five-inch cards or paper cut to about that size, pencils, poster boards or construction paper (11"×17" or 18"×24"); one for each two families—scissors, glue sticks, copies of the four hand-outs (p. 191–194); if you choose the alternate warm-up—a piece of craft wire (similar to telephone wire) or a long pipe cleaner for each participant

1. Warm-up: Each family gets a three-by-five-inch card or other piece of paper and a pencil. Ask them to write their family's name vertically along the long side of the card or paper and then use each letter of the name to start a word or phrase that describes the family. Allow a few minutes for everyone to work on this. If you wander and listen as they are working, you will see and hear interesting things about the families in your group—what they are writing but more importantly, how they are deciding, discussing and interacting.

   Invite families to share what they have written by reading their card out loud if they wish.

   Alternate Warm-up: Give each individual a craft wire or a long pipe cleaner and ask them each to make something that tells something about their family. Next, have them talk about their creations and join them together into a family sculpture.

2. Give out the first of the four hand-outs. Ask families to read the text on the top out loud, cut the pages as indicated, take time to think and write their personal answers to the question posed on the hand-out (younger members may need help writing or spelling) and then share their answers out loud with one another. Participants should hold onto their texts (top part of hand-out) and writings (the little cut-outs with their answers).

   Repeat this four times (once with each sheet).

3. Give each family a poster board or similar surface on which they create a family collage using all their writings and the four texts. (If you chose the alternate warm-up, it may be possible to incorporate the family sculpture into the collage as well.) Ask families to give their collage a title.

4. Culminate with a "gallery walk,"[5] or have pairs or trios of families meet in small groups to explain and show to each other what their collaboration looks like.

---

[5]Tape all the collages up on the walls of the room (or set them out on tables). Participants can walk around and study everyone else's production.

Outdoor Adventures for the Family

These are family outdoor experiences that provide each family with an interactive experience with the natural world. Each of these is designed to begin as a community gathering of all the families, after which families go off on their own and then regroup to share their findings with one another.

1. As families gather, the song leader can lead an informal sing-down-type activity in which people suggest songs that mention trees, flowers, colors, animals or other outdoor categories.

2. Send families off with whatever supplies they need. Announce a time frame (twenty minutes is probably sufficient for these activities) and let them know what sound to listen for (whistle, gong), which will tell them to return because time is up.

3. Close with some kind of structured sharing of some of the things that families found. Who found the biggest letter alef? Who found an interesting letter lamed? How many greens did you locate?

    This is a great time to teach a *berakha* (blessing) related to the beauties of nature and talk a little bit about the beautiful things that God has put in the world for us to enjoy.

4. Finish with some more outdoor songs.

The Great Alef-Bet Hunt

Families receive a chart with the letters of the Hebrew alphabet. Their assignment is to see how many things in nature they can spot (sketch) or find (collect) that look like letters of the alphabet.

Supplies: Hand-outs (see p. 188) and Ziploc bags

The Family Scavenger Hunt

Each family receives a list of things to look for.
Supplies: Hand-out (p. 189) and Ziploc bags

Rock and Stroll

A self-contained step-by-step adventure that involves finding and getting to know a pet rock, then decorating it and adopting it.

Supplies: Hand-out (p. 190), art supplies for decorating the rocks at the close of the activity

The Green Machine

Give each family a handful of green paint chips (of the sort available at paint stores) and send them off to find things that match each different shade of green.

Supplies: Lots of paint chips (collect for months before your program) and some clear tape for taping down "specimens"

Take a Closer Look

Give each family a string or ribbon about eighteen inches long. Ask them to walk out at least five minutes' distance from the meeting place and place their string on the ground in the form of a circle, square or triangle (so that it encloses an area). Ask them to study their territory and make a list of all the things they see within their string boundaries. It helps if you can make available some sort of magnifying glass for each family, too.

Supplies: Lengths of string, pencils, paper, magnifying glasses (you can probably borrow some from a community preschool or day school, or there are plastic pocket lenses available for about $1.50 each; families can also work in pairs and share the lens)

Parent Orientation Meeting

It is important to schedule a parent orientation meeting very near the beginning of the retreat, because even if you have put many of the nitty-gritty details in writing (see a sample of such a hand-out on p. 155), parents will still need to ask questions and have the important information reinforced.

Do not be surprised by the levels of anxiety expressed by parents in this kind of new setting. They need to be reassured that the planners of the retreat have considered the details and planned carefully and are concerned first and foremost with the children's safety.

On a weekend retreat that begins Friday evening, it is very hard to find time for this meeting at the beginning of the retreat. You will feel yourself hurtling toward Shabbat and will probably consider yourself fortunate if the families and staff have all *arrived* by Shabbat. We have always tried to squeeze in a very short (fifteen minutes) meeting before candlelighting, during which we also emphasize taking the time to read the "required reading for parents" in their folders. Later, after the kids are asleep, we have some time either before or after the parents' evening program to answer questions and mention any other critical details.

On a longer camp session (which might begin on a weekday with lunch), we schedule an orientation session for the first afternoon, when the kids are at their first group session. We try to keep it to half an hour so adult study sessions can get off the ground on that first afternoon. When there is a mixture of returning families and first-time families, you might divide up into two separate orientation meetings.

Outline for a Parent Orientation Meeting

1. Welcome.

2. Introduce key staff people.

3. Give overview of schedule.

4. Clarify issue of responsibility for children—who is responsible for kids when—and the safeguards in place to help that work (that is, when and where to deliver kids to counselors and pick them up; reminder to let counselors know if their child is not joining the group, and so on).

5. The shmirah system—how the evening babysitting works.

6. A brief composite sketch of the counselors as a group; what to do if a problem arises (your child has a complaint about the counselor, you observe something that you think is problematic).

7. General health and safety issues pertaining to your site and the season of the year (drink water, wear sun hat and sunscreen, and so on); introduce doctor/nurse; give location of first aid kits, ice

machine (for bruises and bee stings), phones that can dial 911, nearest emergency hospital).

8. Site-specific safety rules such as no bare feet, no kids in a rowboat without an adult, no one in a boat without a life jacket.

9. Fire evacuation procedures: It is important to stress that the staff knows what to do and will bring kids to the meeting/evacuation place; parents *must not* go looking for their kids.

10. Pool: Lifeguard's name; any special rules/cautions.

11. What to do if there is a need for a repair in a room, cabin, tent or public area.

12. Meal routines: Will meals begin and end with communal singing or reciting of blessings? Are meals buffet? Are you asking families to sit together? Will there be seating assignments for some meals?

13. Any questions?

Orientation Folder

What to Include
What is the very basic information that people need to orient them to the retreat at the beginning?

- Nametags: If you are using the peel-off-backing kind, put three for *each* family member into the folder—this is so that everyone has one for Erev Shabbat, one for Shabbat[6] and one for Sunday (if still needed). Often, the counselors make special nametags for their group members, which they give out at first group meeting. In that case, just include adult nametags in the folder. If you use the sturdier, more expensive pin-on nametags, one will be sufficient for the duration.

- Map of the site

- Schedule
  Weekend retreat: A detailed schedule of the whole retreat; because Shabbat begins right away and time is short, the schedule will probably be more or less fixed, subject only to minor deviations, which can be announced (p. 148).
  A longer camp: Include an overview schedule and then you can print a more detailed daily schedule (p. 145).

- Explanatory memo that explains various details or basics about the retreat setup; this might include brief notations about kashrut, tefilla and Shabbat; how the shmira (babysitting system) works in the evenings; safety precautions unique to the site; and so on (p. 155).

- List of participants and where they are housed in camp (so they can find someone they are looking for)

- List of kids by groups with counselors' names

In an Outreach Setting
- The local Jewish community newspaper
- The local guide to the Jewish community
- Flyers for upcoming community events

Optional
- Glossary of terms such as *Shabbat Shalom, Shavua Tov, Havdalah, tefilla, shmira, madrikhim* and so on (p. 154)
- Explanatory overview about Shabbat (p. 171)

---

[6]This avoids the writing-on-Shabbat issue posed by lost or unreusable nametags.

- Story for bedtime

What Can Be Added in the Middle of the Retreat
- Study materials given out at the study sessions
- Text for Erev Shabbat celebration (candlelighting berakhot through Birkat haMazon) on the table on Friday night

What to Add at the End of the Retreat
- List of all participants with names of all family members, addresses and phone numbers
- List of all staff members with addresses and phone numbers
- Flyer announcing the reunion
- Copies of all hand-outs used during the retreat, including song sheets, tefilla sheet and Birkat haMazon

11 Hand-Outs

Flyer   129
Newspaper advertisements   130–131
Precamp communications with families   132–139
Precamp communications to counselors   141–144
Overview schedules
    A Tuesday-through-Sunday camp   145
    A Wednesday-through-Sunday camp   146–147
    Weekend retreat schedules   148–150
Arrival hand-outs (in orientation packet)
    Kids' group lists   151–152
    Counselor assignments to groups   153
    Glossary for parents   154
    Parents' introduction to Shabbat Camp (five-day camp)   155–157
Daily schedules and newsletters   158–170
Pre-Shabbat hand-out   171–173
A Shabbat schedule   174
Program hand-outs
    Saturday night pre-Selihot program outline   175
    A Birkat HaMazon story   176
    Rosh HaShana family letter   177–178
    "Family Stuff" sentence completions   179
    A getting-to-know-you bingo game   180
    "Family Stuff" paragraphs
       Version 1   181–182
       Version 2   183
       Footnotes   184
    "The Generations"   185
    "Lost in the Forest"   186
    Recipe for bubbles   187
    Outdoor activities
       Alef Bet Hike   188
       Scavenger Hike   189
       Rock and Stroll   190
    Family Talk Collage   191–194
    Family Camp songs   195–196
A Birkat haMazon   197

A Kabbalat Shabbat tefilla sheet   198
Memos and notes to counselors
   Two-page overview memo   199-200
   Games suggested for a rainy weekend   201-203
Why Evaluation?   204
Evaluation questionnaires   205-216

• friends • Shabbat • study • Shabbat • study • games • prayer • celebration • sun • fun • friends • Shabbat • study • programs for kids • celebration • hikes • stories • dancing • singing • celebration • hikes • programs for adults • programs for kids • fun for parents and kids together

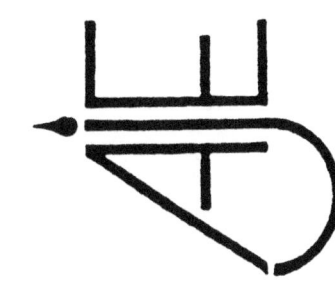

come to **Play, Learn and Celebrate** Shabbat with us at the East Bay's

Jewish Family Camp Weekend

Nov. 10-Nov. 12

at a retreat site in the Napa hills

for information call Janet Harris or Vicky Kelman at the Agency for Jewish Education*: **839-2900**

This program has been made possible by a grant from the Koret Foundation and the Endowment Foundation of the Jewish Federation of the Greater East Bay.

*an agency of the Jewish Federation of the Greater East Bay

• programs for adults • programs for kids • fun for parents and kids together •

come to **Play,**
Learn and **Celebrate**
Shabbat with us at the
East Bay's first

Jewish Family Camp Weekend

February 10 – February 12
and
May 12 – May 14
at a retreat site in the Napa hills

for information call Janet Harris or Vicky Kelman
at the Agency for Jewish Education*:   **533-7462**

This program has been made possible by a grant from the Koret Foundation and the Endowment Foundation of the Jewish Federation of the Greater East Bay.
*an agency of the Jewish Federation of the Greater East Bay

• prayer • celebration • sun • fun • friends • Shabbat • study • programs for • kids • celebration • singing • dancing • stories • hikes • friends • Shabbat • study • Shabbat • study • games •

the ultimate family vacation!

Ramah Family Camp

Wednesday, August 29 through Monday, September 3

a unique opportunity:
- to study, celebrate and worship as part of a dynamic Jewish community
- to enrich the life of your family
- to experience Judaism as a source of nurture and renewal for family life

and a chance to:
- swim, play tennis, hike, dance and sing

programs for adults . . . programs for kids . . . and programs for adults and kids together

for applications and more information, call our office: 213-476-8571
or write: Camp Ramah, c/o the University of Judaism
15600 Mulholland Drive, Los Angeles, CA 90077

Camp Ramah is located at the Max and Pauline Zimmer Conference Center of the University of Judaism in Ojai, California. Camp Ramah in California operates under the educational auspices of the University of Judaism.

Agency for Jewish Education *of the Greater East Bay*

Rabbi Stuart Kelman, Ph.D.
Executive Director

David Gould
Chair

Richard Goodman
Vice Chair

Marcia Nord
Secretary

Roger Wilson
Treasurer

Robert Stamper
Immediate Past Chair

Susan Agron
Ernest Alexander
Helene Barkin
Diane Bernbaum
Daniel Bloom
Rabbi Ira Book
Jack Clauson
Karen Harley
Peter Jacobi
Joan Sopher
Ernst Valfer
Rolf Weinberg

Seymour Fromer
Founding Director

"Learning - learning - learning: that is the secret of Jewish survival"

Ahad HaAm, in a letter to J.L. Magnes

WHAT IS SHABBAT CAMP???
A PLACE FOR FAMILIES TO BE JEWISH TOGETHER...

THERE ARE PROGRAMS FOR PARENTS AND CHILDREN TOGETHER, FOR PARENTS TO STUDY AND LEARN WITH EACH OTHER, FOR KIDS TO PLAY AND DISCOVER TOGETHER. ACTIVITIES INCLUDE SINGING, DANCING, CRAFTS, NATURE HIKES, STUDY, STORYTELLING, SERVICES, AND MORE.

WHEN IS SHABBAT CAMP???

SHABBAT CAMP BEGINS AT 3:00 P.M. FRIDAY AFTERNOON, MAY 12TH. WE ENCOURAGE FAMILIES TO GET THERE AS CLOSE TO THAT TIME AS POSSIBLE, SO THAT WE MAY BEGIN SHABBAT PREPARATIONS. WE WILL CONCLUDE AT APPROXIMATELY 2:00 P.M. ON SUNDAY AFTERNOON.

WHO COMES TO SHABBAT CAMP???

BOTH SINGLE AND DUAL PARENT FAMILIES, GRANDPARENTS, AND CHILDREN BETWEEN THE AGES OF BIRTH AND TWELVE HAVE PARTICIPATED IN SHABBAT CAMP. WE HAVE NO FORMAL PROGRAM FOR CHILDREN UNDER THE AGE OF THREE..
APPROXIMATELY 12-15 FAMILIES WILL BE AT SHABBAT CAMP. STAFF CONSISTS OF TWO CAMP CO-ORDINATORS, A COOK, A MUSIC SPECIALIST, AS WELL AS CAREFULLY SELECTED TEENAGERS, WHO ARE COUNSELORS, WHO HAVE PARTICIPATED IN THE AGENCY FOR JEWISH EDUCATIONS EDUCATIONAL PROGRAMS.

WHERE IS SHABBAT CAMP???

SHABBAT CAMP IS HELD AT ENCHANTED HILLS, A SUMMER CAMP OPERATED BY THE LIGHTHOUSE FOR THE BLIND. IT IS APPROXIMATELY ONE AND A HALF HOURS FROM OAKLAND, LOCATED IN THE NAPA HILLS. HOUSING CONSISTS OF EITHER SELF-CONTAINED CABINS WHICH SLEEP 4-5 PEOPLE AND HAVE A PRIVATE BATH. THERE ARE ALSO ROOMS IN A LODGE WITH SHARED BATHROOMS. ALL ACCOMODATIONS ARE HEATED. ENCHANTED HILLS IS A BEAUTIFUL FACILITY-THERE IS A POND WITH DUCKS AND GEESE, A VIEW OF THE SURROUNDING HILLS, A MULTI-SENSORY PLAYGROUND, HORSES TO PET AND FEED, HIKING TRAILS, AND SEVERAL AVIARIES.

FOOD

ALL MEALS WILL BE KOSHER, AND PREPARED BY THE AGENCY FOR JEWISH EDUCATION STAFF. WITH THE EXCEPTION OF FRIDAY NIGHT, ALL MEALS WILL BE VEGETARIAN. PLENTIFUL SNACKS WILL BE PROVIDED.

COST: $105.00 PER ADULT, $85.00 CHILDREN OVER THREE, $25.00 CHILDREN UNDER THREE. ($5.00 REDUCTION EACH SUCCESSIVE CHILD)

FOR INFORMATION AND REGISTRATION

CALL THE AGENCY FOR JEWISH EDUCATION, AT 839-2900, AND ASK FOR JANET HARRIS OR VICKY KELMAN.

---

401 Grand Avenue   Oakland, California 94610   (415) 839-2900   FAX (415) 839-3996

An Agency of the Jewish Federation of the Greater East Bay

Agency for Jewish Education *of the Greater East Bay*

Rabbi Stuart Kelman, Ph.D.
Executive Director

June 4, 1990 / 11 Sivan 5750

David Gould
Chair

Karen Harley
V. Chair

Marcia Nord
Secretary

Roger Wilson
Treasurer

Robert Stamper
Immediate Past Chair

Susan Agron
Ernest Alexander
Elaine Bachrach
Diane Bernbaum
Daniel Bloom
Rabbi Ira Book
Jack Clauson
 d Friedkin
Herb Friedman
Richard Goodman
Peter Jacobi
Lawrence Katz
Cindy Levitas
Jackie Mintz
Ruth Morris
Paul Sieger
Karla Smith
Ernst Valter
Rolf Weinberg

Seymour Fromer
Founding Director

Learning learning
earning that is the
secret of Jewish
 val

 ad Ha'Am, in a letter
 J.L. Magnes

Dear Campers,

We're delighted that you'll be joining us and we look forward to seeing you on Wednesday afternoon, June 20 - as close to 12:30 p.m. as possible.

Our Shabbat Camp will be held at Enchanted Hills Camp, 3410 Mt. Veeder Road, Napa. It is a beautiful camp facility owned by the Lighthouse for the Blind of San Francisco. It is used in the summer as a camp for the blind and visually impaired.

Here are some of the things you'll need to know to prepare for the weekend:

Housing:

Each family will be housed in heated facilities - either a cabin with two adjoining rooms and a bathroom, or in a lodge room (shared bathrooms along a central hallway). Bring your own pillows, toiletries (including soap), bed linens (twin size) or sleeping bags, and towels. If you have a child who requires a crib, plan to bring your own.

Meals:

We will be eating 12 meals together from Wednesday lunch through lunch on Sunday June 24. All meals will be kosher. We will serve a meat meal on Friday night and most other meals will be vegetarian. Plentiful snacks are provided. If you will be bringing additional snacks for your family, or baby food, please make sure that everything is vegetarian. (This means nothing with any animal or shellfish ingredients. Baked goods should specify 100% vegetable shortening on the label.)

What to Bring:

This is camp - so dress is casual. For Friday night please bring a white shirt or blouse for you and your children.
In addition to bedding as described above and whatever clothing your family requires for the weekend, be sure to include:

1. Warm jacket (hat and mittens if you have them) evenings can get quite chilly.

2. Guitar or other sing-a-long instrument if you play one.

3. Rain gear - just in case.

4. Any sports equipment your family enjoys using

401 Grand Avenue   Oakland, California 94610   (415) 839-2900   FAX (415) 839-3996
An Agency of the Jewish Federation of the Greater East Bay

5. Flashlights

6. Kippah, tallit and tefillin if you have them

7. Shabbat candles and candle holders (we'll also have lots available)

8. Optional for families with toddlers: a stroller (distances are <u>very</u> short, but paths <u>are</u> paved), sassy seat

9. Bathing suits (there is a swimming pool)

10. Sun screen and sun hat

Odds and Ends:

We do have a nurse on our staff. Should there be a need for additional medical help we are about 20 minutes from Queen of the Valley Hospital in Napa.

Should anyone need to reach you, the emergency phone number at Enchanted Hills is 1-707-224-4023. This is an answering machine which is checked several times a day. There is a pay phone on the grounds should you need to make a call.

Program Overview:

We plan to start at 1:00 p.m. on Wednesday with lunch. Our afternoon will be a getting-acquainted time, with lots of singing, a family swim, and games. Dinner will be at 6:15 followed by a family evening activity. Our adult session, as well as evening babysitting, begins at 9:30.

Our mornings begin with an 8:00 a.m. breakfast and include group services, then separate sessions for adults and children.

The afternoons are a combination of family time and time when children are with counselors and adults have their own programming. There is also plenty of leisure time for both adults and kids! Also, the pool will be open and we will have an "open art studio" featuring different media each day.

Shabbat, of course, will have its own special flavor. We will begin Shabbat preparations on Friday afternoon by making challah - and more.

We're looking forward to meeting you. . . . . .

Vicky

Janet Harris   Vicky Kelman

Agency for Jewish Education *of the Greater East Bay*

Rabbi Stuart Kelman, Ph.D.
Executive Director

David Gould
Chair

Karen Harley
Vice Chair

Marcia Nord
Secretary

Roger Wilson
Treasurer

Robert Stamper
Immediate Past Chair

Susan Agron
Ernest Alexander
Elaine Bachrach
Diane Bernbaum
Daniel Bloom
Rabbi Ira Book
Jack Clauson
Gerald Friedkin
Herb Friedman
Richard Goodman
Peter Jacobi
Lawrence Katz
Cindy Levitas
Jackie Mintz
Ruth Morris
Paul Siegel
Karla Smith
Ernst Valter
Rolf Weinberg

Seymour Fromer
Founding Director

June 12, 1990 / 19 Silvan 5750

Dear Campers,

We are eagerly anticipating camp next week. Here are a few last minute reminders:

Plan to arrive between 11:30 and 12:30 on Wednesday, June 20.

Please leave bicycles, skateboards and electronic toys at home.

Bring enough clothes to last through Sunday - including a white shirt or blouse for Shabbat.

Call if you have any questions, concerns, etc.

We will be at camp on Tuesday night. The number is 1-707-224-4023. You may also call the AJE at 839-2900 and ask for Doris or Stuart.

We haven't yet experienced summer at Enchanted Hills. You may wish to bring a portable fan if there is a hot spell.

L'hitraot

Janet and Vicky

campjune

401 Grand Avenue   Oakland, California 94610   (415) 839-2900   FAX (415) 839-3996
An Agency of the Jewish Federation of the Greater East Bay

7 July 1991

Dear Family Camp Family,

Preparations for Family Camp are in full swing and although the first session of family camp is still about six weeks away we are already feeling a surge of anticipation and enthusiasm. We hope you are feeling the same way.

At this point, we are putting the finishing touches on our staff. Those of you who are returning will find both friendly familiar faces and friendly new faces among our faculty and counselors. If this is your first Ramah Family Camp experience you are about to meet an amazing array of new people and make many new friends. We are all energetically planning for a stimulating and fun five days at camp.

△△△△△

One of the programs we're planning is a special Family Camp wrap-up-the-outgoing-Jewish-year and start-the-new-one-off **Tzedakah*** project. If this sounds like something your family would like to participate in, please get ready by setting aside the pennies left in your pockets (purse, lunchbox, briefcase, etc.,) daily between now and Family Camp. Bring your family penny collection with you when you come to camp

△△△△△

Please plan to arrive at camp between 10 and 11:30 a.m. on your first day (21 August for first session and 27 August for second session). Our first "offical event" will be lunch at 12:30.

You will be receiving one more letter from us before camp. It will arrive during the first week in August and will contain details about what to bring (and what to leave home) along with driving instructions to camp.

Remember --- if you have any questions at all, please don't hesitate to call Yael Schnall at the camp office (805) 646-4301 or call me at directly at my home in Berkeley (415) 524-5886.

I am looking forward to meeting you at camp.....

Vicky
Vicky Kelman
Family Camp Director

* social justice, repairing the world

CAMP RAMAH IN CALIFORNIA
At the Max & Pauline Zimmer Conference Center

Mannon Kaplan
President

Jake Farber
Chairman of the Board

Rabbi Edward M. Feinstein
Executive Director

Diane Cohen
Director of Development

Yael Goss
Program Director

Elie Mechaly
Operations Manager

7 August 1991

Dear Family Camp Family,

It's almost time.....Here is your last minute briefing:

1. Things to bring:

Δ We're not sending a clothing list. You're the best judge of what your family members will need for five days at camp. Keep in mind that Ojai is usually hot and dry at this time of year but evenings are often cool enough for a sweater or sweatshirt.

Bring something white to wear for Friday night if you already have it. (Don't buy anything special just for camp.) The wearing of white really seems to add to the Shabbat astmosphere. In any case, plan to something more more than ordinary camp clothes. We suggest a skirt for women and girls, sportshirts for men and boys. Shabbat morning at Ramah is more casual than Friday night but a step up from jeans and t-shirts.

Δ If you will be in either deluxe housing, Ramah will be providing sheets, blankets and towels. If you are in standard housing (a cabin) please bring bedding(sleeping bags are fine) and towels for your children. They will be provided for adults. If you are in rustic housing please bring bedding(sleeping bags are great) and towels for all. We suggest that everyone bring additional beach towels for use at the pool.

Δ Bring a flashlight.

Δ If you need a porta-crib or highchair, please bring your own. We do not have any at camp. In general, families with children 2 and under do find it helpful to have a stroller at camp (although distances are not great).

Δ It would be a good idea for those living in rustic housing to bring something in which to carry shower stuff (soap, shampoo, etc.,) to and from the showers. (Our summer campers and staff use children's plastic beach pails or small plastic buckets.)

Δ If you are living in standard or rustic housing, bring a fan if you have one. It can be a very helpful thing to have in the event of a heatwave.

Δ Bring kipot or other head covering as well as Tallit and Tefillin if you own them. We will have Shabbat candle holders for all but you might wish to bring your own.

Δ If you play the guitar, banjo, fiddle or other such instrument, bring it along! We hope to have time (formal and informal) to sing together.

Δ Be sure to bring sunhats and sunscreen for your family members.

15600 Mulholland Drive, Los Angeles, California 90077 Telephone 213 476-8571 Fax 213 472-3810

Δ If you have a 2 - 5 year old, please bring a backpack or diaper bag clearly labelled with your child's name.

2. things to leave at home:

Δ skateboards, kids' bicycles (and other riding toys) and electronic games

3. Laundry:

ΔThere are laundry facilities at camp with several washers and dryers. If you expect you'll need to do laundry, bring lots of quarters (a load of wash requires 3 quarters and a dryer cycle requires 2) and detergent.

4. Food:

Δ We will be serving three meals and snacks everyday. If you bring additional snacks for your family, please adhere to Ramah's kashrut policy which means bring nothing which is meat or of animal origin, or contains either. Homemade baked goods must come from a kosher home. Packaged and processed foods should clearly specify the use of 100% vegetable shortening. No food may be brought into the diningroom.

5. Telephone:

Δ Ramah's phone number is: (805) 646-4301. We will have an administrative assistant in the office who will be answering calls during the day. Should you receive a phone call, the message will be delivered to you at the next meal.

Δ We also have an answering service which handles all phone calls which come in while the office is closed. Messages which come in overnight are collected first thing in the morning.

Δ There are three conveniently located pay phones should you need to make any calls.

Δ Δ Δ

Δ Please label kids' stuff that you hope to be able to bring home with you (such as beach towels, bathingsuits, hats, sweatshirts, mitts, bats, etc.,).

Δ And: don't forget to bring your summer penny harvest for our family camp tzedakah project!!!!

Δ Δ Δ

Driving instructions to Camp Ramah:

from Southern California: take the Ventura Freeway (101) West to route 33 (just past Ventura)

from Northern California: take 101 south to route 33 (which is just before Ventura) or, take route 5 south to 126 (west) to the 101 (north toward Santa Barbara) to route 33 (which is just a few exits north)

Stay on route 33 for about 13 miles to Ojai. When route 33 turns left, make the turn and stay with it (now also called Maricopa Highway) for about 1 1/2 miles. Take a right on Fairview Road and continue about 1/4 mile uphill to Ramah which will be on your left. The first thing you will see is a large carved stone sign which reads: the Max and Pauline Zimmer Conference Center of the University of Judaism. Drive on in. Our friendly greeters will let you know what to do next!

Plan to arrive by about 11:00/ 11:30 so that you can be unpacked and ready for lunch (our first "official" activity) at 12:30.

∆ ∆ ∆

We look forward to welcoming you to Family Camp!

Vicky

Vicky Kelman
Family Camp Director

P.S. From the 12th on, you can reach me at camp: 805-646-4301. Don't hesitate to call with any questions or concerns.

Keep collecting those pennies!!!

CAMP RAMAH IN CALIFORNIA
At the Max & Pauline Zimmer Conference Center

Mannon Kaplan
President

Jake Farber
Chairman of the Board

Rabbi Edward M. Feinstein
Executive Director

Diane Cohen
Director of Development

Yael Goss
Program Director

Elie Mechaly
Operations Manager

30 May 1991

Dear

As you may know, I am the director of the Family Camp at Camp Ramah in Ojai, California. As its name suggests, family camp is a Jewish camping experience for families. Families come and live together (in rooms or bunks or tents, according to their own choice), joining in the community of families for experiences such as tefilla every morning, singing and evening programs. Certain portions of the day (in previous years, about 3 1/2 hours in the morning and about 1 1/2 hours in the afternoon) we have age-group programming during which children play and study with their peers and the adults get an opportunity to do the same.

I am in the process of seeking a few additional staff members for the coming summer and I would like to extend an invitation to you to join our staff.

Here are the relevant details: *

Δ Camp Ramah is located in Ojai California, which is between Ventura and Santa Barbara (inland about 20 minutes from Highway 101)

Δ There are two sessions of Family Camp:
session #1: 25 -27 August (We'd need you from dinner time on the 24th until 2 pm on the 27th.)
session #2: 27 August - 1 September (We'd need you from dinner on the 26th until 2 pm on the 1st.)

Δ We would like you to join our staff for either or both sessions (clearly, there's time off between the sessions).

---

* -- if this appeals to you and is possible given the limitations of your academic and personal life, please return the enclosed and we can talk further on the phone or in person:

15600 Mulholland Drive, Los Angeles, California 90077 Telephone 213 476 8571 Fax 213 472 3810

Δ Your responsibilities would include primarily:
- responsibility for a group of children during most of the morning and part of the afternoon. You are part of a staff of 3 or 4 counselors who work together to plan and lead activities for your group.
- sharing responsibility for 'shmira' (while the kids are sleeping) in the later evening during the adult evening activity
- facilitating at large group activities such as tefilla and evening programs
- taking a shift helping the life- guard at the pool during the most crowded times

Δ You would be housed with other counselors and would eat some meals with other staff and some mixed in among the families.

Δ Your Honorarium would be $150.00 per session

One more thing -- it's fun!!! Most of our counselors find this a refreshing educational environment to work in and a new way to view camp, education and family life.

Hope you can join us!!!

15 July 1991

CAMP RAMAH IN CALIFORNIA
At the Max & Pauline Zimmer Conference Center

Mannon Kaplan
President

Jake Farber
Chairman of the Board

Rabbi Edward M. Feinstein
Executive Director

Diane Cohen
Director of Development

Yael Goss
Program Director

Elie Mechaly
Operations Manager

Dear

I'm delighted that you'll be joining the staff of Ramah Family Camp 1991 for session #1 / session #2.

If you're working session #1, please plan to be unpacked and ready to begin work at 6:00 pm on Tuesday evening, 20 August. We will have dinner together as a staff and then have the evening and some time the next morning for meetings and preparation. Families will begin arriving at about mid-morning on Wednesday and everything will officially begin with lunch on Wednesday. The session will wrap up by about 2:00 pm on Sunday.

If you are working session #2, please be in camp and ready to begin by 6:00pm on Monday evening, 26 August. That gives us the evening for meetings and preparation. Families will be arriving during the morning on Tuesday and camp officially begins with Tuesday lunch. Our closing celebration is over by about 1:00 pm on Sunday and you can count on being able to leave by about 2:00 pm.

If you are working for both sessions you will have the in-between time (about 28 hours) as a day off.

If you are going to need a ride to camp or an airport pick-up, please let me know (call or drop me a line) and I will do my best to help you get to camp.

I will be available at home for the rest of the summer (except for one week in Yosemite at the very end of July). If you have any questions, don't hesitate to call me: (415) 524-5886. You can reach me <u>at camp</u> after 12 August.

You can expect another letter from me with any last minute information and details by about 10 August.

ΔΔ We have asked all the families who are coming to save their extra pennies for a special wrap-up-the-outgoing-Jewish-year-start-the-new-one-off **tzedakah** project which we will be undertaking during each session. If you'd like to participate, save your pennies from now until camp and bring your penny collection with you to camp.ΔΔ

I'm looking forward to working with you at Family Camp.

15600 Mulhoiland Drive, Los Angeles, California 90077 Telephone 213 476 8571 Fax 213 472 3810

CAMP RAMAH IN CALIFORNIA
At the Max & Pauline Zimmer Conference Center

Mannon Kaplan
President

Jake Farber
Chairman of the Board

Rabbi Edward M. Feinstein
Executive Director

Diane Cohen
Director of Development

Yael Goss
Program Director

Elie Mechaly
Operations Manager

12 August 1991

Dear Family Camp counselor,

Just a few last minute notes:

Please bring bedding (sleeping bag or blankets, sheets, etc.,), pillow and towels.

Don't forget: sunhat, sunscreen, flashlight, watch and alarm clock.

    and: kipah, tallit and tefillin

    and: energy, creativity and smiles!!

When you arrive, check in with me. I'll be in the office. If you're coming for first session, plan to be moved in and ready to start by 6:00 pm on Tuesday evening, 20 August. For second session we will begin at 6:00 pm on Monday, 26 August. If you are working for both sessions you will have a day off in between sessions. (You are welcome to stay in camp if you wish.) Both sessions will conclude by about 2:00pm on Sunday (the 25th and the 1st).

If you have any questions or need any more information, you can reach me at camp: (805) 646-4301.

See you soon!

Vicky

remember to keep "harvesting" your pennies

15600 Mulholland Drive, Los Angeles, California 90077 Telephone 213 476-8571 Fax 213 472 3810

FAMILY CAMP
an overview of the week
(you will receive a separate detailed schedule each day)

Tuesday	Wednesday	Thursday	Erev שבת shabbat	shabbat שבת	sunday
arrive and unpack	8:15 breakfast 9- tefilla 9:30-12:45 Kids with counselors and groups 9:30-10:30 parents' free time 11-12:45 parents study and singing	8:15 breakfast 9- tefilla 9:30-12:45 Kids with counselors and groups 9:30-10:30 parents' free time 11-12:45 parents study and singing	8:15 breakfast 8:45 family hallah making 9:30-10 tefilla 10:-12:45 Kids' group time 10-11 freetime 11-12:45 parents study and singing	8:30 breakfast 9:15 tefilla (and Torahreading) kiddush Kids group time / parents study time	6am - trip to Lake Casitas 8:45 tefilla or b'kfst at 8:00 9:15 - Kids'/ adult grouptime, study special "wrap-up" preparations 12- Closing Celebration!
12:30 lunch	1:00 lunch	1:00 lunch	1:00 lunch	lunch 1:00	bag lunches for the road
1:30 singing, orientation, meet your counselors 2:30-3:30 FAMILY SWIM 3:45 snack 4-6 Kids' groups meet / 4-4:45 parents' meeting / 4:45-5:45 parents study groups 5:45 singing	1:45-3 REST 3-4:30 Kids with counselors and groups 4:30-5:30 FAMILY TIME 5:45 singing for all	1:45-3 REST 3-4:30 Kids with counselors and groups 4:30-5:30 FAMILY TIME 5:45 singing for all	1:15-3 REST 3-4:30 Kids' grouptime (shabbat prep) / parents' pre-Shabbat activities 4:30 families prep for Shabbat Kabbalat Shabbat	REST pool opens at 3:00 FAMILY SHABBAT TIME singing, dancing, etc, swimming 6:15 Seudah shlishit	SHALOM L'HITRAOT שלום ולהתראות שנה טובה shana tova safe journey 1991
6:15 dinner	6:15 dinner	6:15 dinner	Shabbat dinner ONEG SHABBAT FOR ALL Cheverim & Shemesh oneg shabbat	7:15 family fun night 8:15 havdallah Shemesh & Haverim	
6 7-8 family evening program 8- Chaverim & Shemesh evening program 9:30-11 parents evening program	7-8 family evening program 8- Chaverim & Shemesh evening program 9:30-11 parents evening program	7-8 family evening program 8- Chaverim & Shemesh evening program 9:30-11 parents evening program	9:30-11 parents evening program	10-11:30 parents evening program	

FAMILY CAMP
an overview of the week
(you will receive a separate detailed schedule each day)

Wednesd 21	Thursday 22	Erev ערב shabbat Aug 23	Shabbat שבת Aug 24	Sunday Aug 25
arrive an unpa	8: breakfast	8 breakfast	8:30 breakfast	6 am - trip to Lake Casitas
	9 - tefilla	8:45 family hallah making	9:15 tefilla (and Torahreading)	8+5 - tefilla
	9:30-12:45 Kids with counselors and groups | 9:30-10:30 parents' free time	9:30-10 tefilla	kiddush	9:15 - Ki Kids' grouptime | adult study
	11-12:45 parents study and singing →	10:-12:45 Kids group time | 10-11 freetime | 11-12:45 parents study and singing →	Kids group time | parents study time	speech/"wrap-up" preparations
12:30 lunch	1:00 lunch	1:00 lunch	lunch 1:00	12 - closing celebration!
1:30 singing, orientation, meet your counselors	1:45-3 REST arts & crafts for FAMILIES	1:45-3 REST arts & crafts for FAMILIES	REST pool opens at 3:00	bag lunches for the road
2:30-3:30 FAMILY SWIM	3-4:30 Kids with counselors and groups	3-4:30 Kids' grouptime (shabbat prep) | parents' pre-Shabbat activities	FAMILY SHABBAT TIME singing, hike, dancing, etc	SHALOM L'HITRA'OT
3:45 snack	4:30-5:30 FAMILY TIME	4:30 families prep for shabbat		לנסיעה טובה safe j'ney
4-6 Kids groups meet | 4-4:45 parents' meeting | 4:45-5:45 parents study groups	5:30 singing	Kabbalat Shabbat	6:15 ev	שנה טובה shana tova
5:45 sin th :5 mer	nner	Shabbat dinner ONEG SHABBAT FOR ALL	7:15 family fun night	
6 | 7-8 family evening program	7-8 family evening program	Chaverim & Shemesh oneg shabbat	8:15 havdallah	
8 - Chaverim & Shemesh evening program	8 - Chaverim & Shemesh evening program		8 - Shemesh & Haverim	
9:30-11 parents evening program	9:30-11 parents evening program	9:30-11 parents evening program	10-11:30 parents evening program	

1991

AJE 5 day Family Shabbat Camp 20-24 June 1990

wednesday	thursday	erev Shabbat	Shabbat	sunday
arrive and unpack	8-8:45 breakfast 9-9:30 tefilla (services) 9:30-12:00 Kids: with their groups and Counselors 9:30-10:30 adults: free time/pool open; discussion with Vanda 10:30-12:00 study session with Jody →	8-8:45 breakfast 9-9:30 tefilla 9:30-12:00 Kids with their groups and Counselors 9:30-10:30 adults: free time/pool open; discussion with Vicky 10:30-12:00 study with Jody →	8-9 breakfast 9:15-10:15 tefilla 10:45 kiddush 10:30-12:30 Kids: with their groups | parents: 10:30-11:30 study with Vicky (this week's Torah portion) free time →	8-9 breakfast and make your picnic sandwiches 9:15-9:45 tefilla 10-11:30 Kids with their groups | parents study and wrap-up 11:30-12:30 pack-up & clean-up 12:30-1:30 PICNIC lunch closing celebration and goodbye circle
12:30 lunch	12:15-1 lunch	12:15-1 lunch	12:30-1:15 lunch	graduation! (we're) in to drive safely!!!
1:15 opening session singing meet counselors 2-3 Family Swim 3:15 snack 3:30-5 Kids: meeting with counselors and first study session | parents: meeting and first study session 5:45-6:15 singing	rest 1-3* 3-4:30 Kids in groups | parents: free time 4:30-5:30 family time 5:45-6:15 singing	1-1:30 family hallah making* 1:30-3 rest* 3-5 getting ready for Shabbat kids in groups | parents: choice of activities 5-6 get showered and dressed for Shabbat 6:00 candlelighting 6:15-6:45 welcoming Shabbat	shabbat rest (pool open 3-4:30 nature walk 3:30-4:30 4:30-6 Kids with their groups | parents' discussion 6-6:30 singing 6:30 third Shabbat meal	*arts and crafts open for "non-happing" children and their parents
dinner 6:15	dinner 6:15	6:45-7:20 dinner 7:30-8:15 Family Shabbat Celebration	7:15-8:15 Family Fun Night 8:15-9 take a family walk 9 havdallah 10 parents' evening program	
7-8 family evening program 9:30-11 adult evening program	7"B family evening program 9:30-11 parent evening program	9:30-11 parents? Oneg Shabbat featuring Brad Burston		

☆ this is an overview— see your daily schedule for places, details and explanations! ☆

*arts and crafts open for "non-happing" children and their parents

watch the moon! something special is happening to it this week....

Shabbat Camp: 30 March – 1 April 1990

Erev Shabbat / Friday

4:00 WELCOME TO SHABBAT CAMP!!!!

    arrive, unpack and get settled; unwind; learn your way around
    make name-tags and Shabbat decorations (dining room)
    meet other families and counselors
    snack

5:30 a very short orientation meeting (dining room)
        followed by
6:00 lighting candles (dining room)
        and
    welcoming Shabbat with songs, stories and prayers (Kiva)

6:45 Shabbat dinner and singing (diningroom)

7:30 an Oneg Shabbat (Shabbat celebration) for the whole family   (diningroom)

8:30 Laila Tov *--- bedtime for kids! Parents put their kids to sleep. Counselors will begin Shmirah (babysitting) at 9:15.

9:30 evening program for parents-- a chance to get better acquainted, talk, laugh and enjoy Shabbat (diningroom)

10:30 refreshments and informal singing

11:00 end of Shmira

                           * * * * * * * * * *

                                          *good-night

Shabbat/ Saturday

8:00 - 9:15 a buffet breakfast is out and ready; come in and help yourself.

9:30 T'fillah -- a Shabbat service for the whole family with singing and Torah reading (Kiva)

10:30 kiddush dining room)

10:45 kids' Shabbat activities with counselors   (til 12:15)

10:45 - 11:45 adults: study session #1 (dining room) **Passover: Passing our story on**

  to 12:15 free time

12:15 Shabbat lunch and singing

1:00 Shabbat menuha (rest) for the family -- naps, relaxation, time for sports, reading, hikes etc.,

3:00 Shabbat activities for the whole family

  3:00 to 3:30 singing with Allison (diningroom)
      sing some old favorites, learn some new favorites, warm up for Passover and get ready to be part of the Havdallah choir
  3:30 to 4:00 a Shabbat nature walk with Annette (meet on the porch of the diningroom)
      or: Get ready for Passover: learn (or review) the 4 questions! with Allison (in the diningroom)

4:00 meet in diningroom
  Kids: Shabbat activities with their groups and counselors*
      ('til 6:00) -- kids will have snack in their groups

  adults: study session #2: 4:00 til 5:15
      choose one of these 2:
        Passover 101 -- Passover for beginners (Vicky)
        or
        the Four children and your children: an in depth study of a page of the Haggadah (Stuart)

      5:15 - 6:00 free time

6:15 -   third Shabbat meal and singing

7:00   havdallah

7:45   family fun night

8:30   Laila Tov kids!

9:30   evening program for parents

11:30   end of Shmira

* * * *

Sunday/ Yom Rishon

8:00   breakfast

8:45   tefilla

9:30 - 11:00   kids: with counselors *

adults: study session #3 **the challenge of being a Jewish family**

11:00 - 12:00   snack: a passover surprise prepared by our kids

and then: our outdoor adventure** :

12:00 - 12:30   pack up

12:30   lunch

1:15   good-bye circle

* kids meet counselors at the end of the **preceeding** activity: on Shabbat -- after kiddush and after and after the Torah roll; Sunday at the end of Tefilla;

** in case of rain, we'll have an indoor adventure --meet in the diningroom!

YEDIDIM (2-5)	KESHET  (6-8)	SHEMESH  (9-11)	CHAVERIM (12-14)
Tyler B.	Brian B	Elysa A	Aaron C
Shira Mayan B	Karen B	David B	David C
~~Ruben Lev B~~	Gabriel Simha B	~~Alissa B~~	~~Yonina~~
Aaron C	Danya C	Liora Ranel B	Eian K
Mark D	Seth F	~~Joshua F~~	Elana K
Lauren D	Jenny F	Josh H →	Joanna R
Levi F	Andrew F	Ilona K	Alyssa R
Jerome F	Noah F	Brandon K	Michael S
Jonathan F	Ariel G	Gabi P	Ronit S
Ariel F	Ethan H	Jonathan R	Havi W
Ilan G	Koby H	Susan R	Tamar Z
Rebecca G	Shannon L	Liat R	
Rebecca H	Sarah L	Haggai R	
Sara K	Ariella L	Gabriel A. R	
Jessica K	Benji P	Jonathan R	
Stephanie K	Damon P	Michael S	
Ari M	Beni R	Ben T	
Alex P	Akiva R	Elana T	
Sandor P	Hilary R	Julie Meira W	
Ari R	Amy R	Michael W	
Elan R	Karen Jael W	~~Tamar Z~~	
Shoshana R	Yoni Z	Carrie S	
Dorit R			
David R			
Jesse R			
Benjamin J. R			
Sammy R			
Talia S			
Erik S			
Benjamin S			
Matthew T			
Aaron W			
Yael Z			
Josh A			

152 Jewish Family Retreats

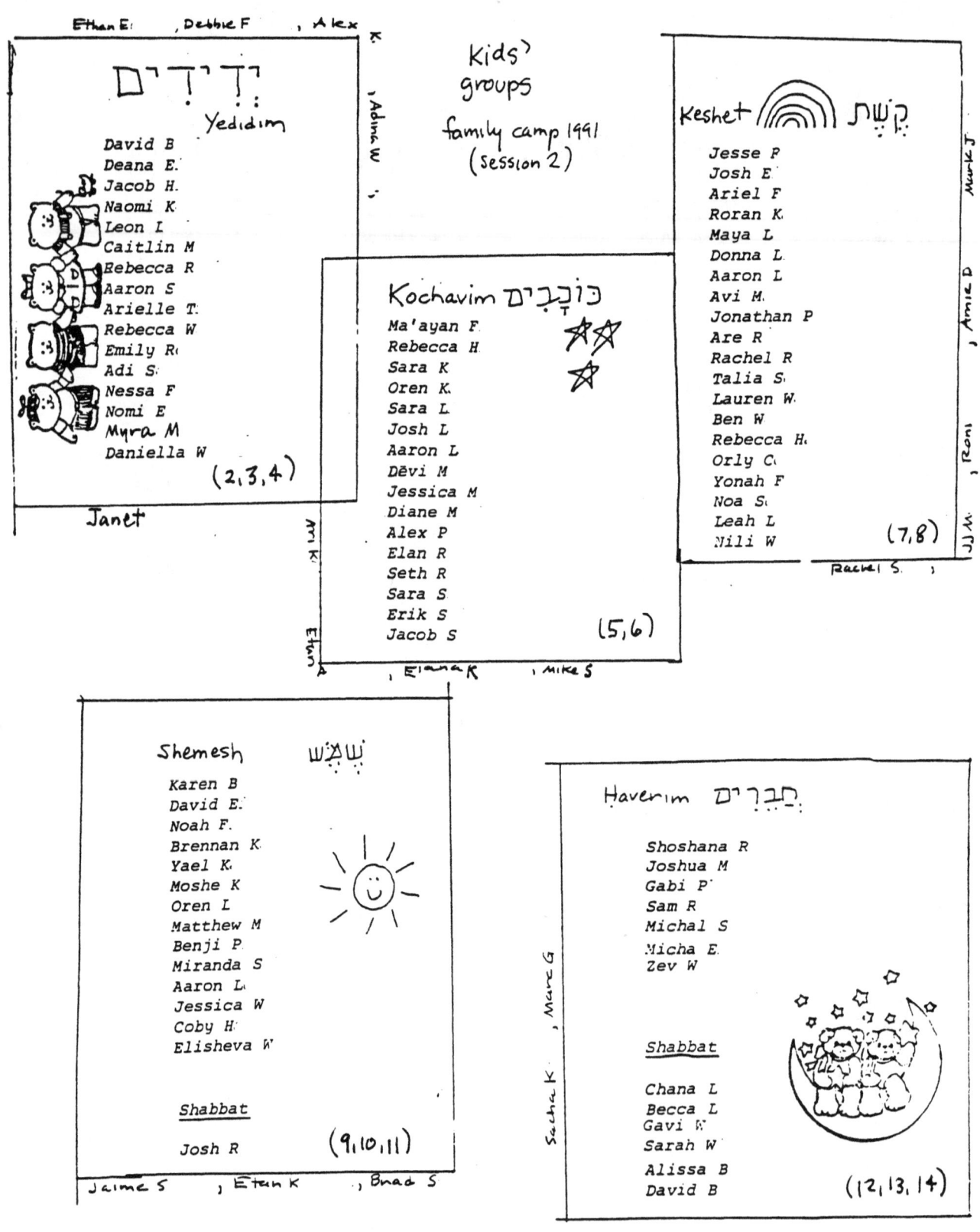

Hand-outs 153

⑭ יְלָדִים
(2-5 yr. olds)

Session #1

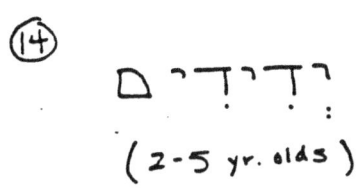 קֶשֶׁת
(6-7)

Danit W.
Ari K
JJ M
Yoni A
Debbie B.

Rachel S
Jordan F.
Etan K

 שֶׁמֶשׁ
(8-9)

חֲבֵרִים
(10-12)

Jaime S.
Elana K.
Etan A

Sacha K
Marc G

A family camp glossary

some common Hebrew words you may hear around camp or see in print here and there:

Hadar Ha Ochel: diningroom

Bet K'nesset: chapel, synagogue

Rikud : (ree - kud) dancing

Shira : (shee-ra) singing

Tefilla: (t- fee-lah) prayer; prayer services;

madrichim: counselors (literally: those who guide the way)

shmira: babysitting (literally --guarding)

hamotzi: the blessing(thank-you) for bread said before meals; (1 sentence)

birkat ha'mazon: the blessing (thank-you) for food said after meals; (1 paragraph and a few short verses, usually sung;)

kashrut: the laws of keeping kosher; in essence: specially slaughtered meat (slaughtered painlessly and with all the blood drained out); all meat and dairy foods (and any products containing either of them) kept completely separate;

Shabbat: Sabbath, the seventh day, Saturday; from sundown on Friday until 3 stars come out on Saturday night;

Erev Shabbat: the eve of the Sabbath; Friday;

Kabbalat Shabbat: welcoming the Shabbat; the Friday evening service

Havdallah: the ceremony marking the end of Shabbat and the start of a new week; (its literal meaning is 'distinction' or 'separation';)

Elul: the last month of the Jewish year (the month we're in now) during which we blow the shofar every day (which alerts us to prepare us for the coming of the new year)

Boker Tov! good morning!   **Laila Tov!** goodnight!

Shabbat Shalom! Have a peaceful Shabbat!

Shavua Tov! Have a good week! (a post-havdallah greeting)

Shanah Tovah! Have a good new year!

If you hear any additional terms which are unfamiliar to you --- please ask!!!!!

A PARENT'S INTRODUCTION TO SHABBAT CAMP

A few helpful things to know:

1. This memo and the schedule are being printed a few days before Shabbat camp begins. Changes in the weather or in the facilities may necessitate schedule or place changes as we go. We'll try to make any changes clear to all through announcements at meals and posted announcements on our announcement board in the diningroom. (Make it a habit to check there before meals.)

2. Most of our programs will take place in and around the diningroom. When in doubt about where to meet -- look there first.

3. Our evening shmirah (babysitting) system works this way: our counselors will be stationed outside in front of the cabins within hearing of all the cabins. In addition, they will 'make rounds' every 5-7 minutes, opening each cabin door to check that all is well. In the lodge, counselors will be in the hallway, checking in on the kids in their rooms. There are 3 counselors assigned to each place (and one 'floater.' There is a counselor from each group -- so you can be sure that a one of your child's counselors is there.

If there is a problem, one of the counselors will come and get you. For this reason it's important that the counselors know where you are. They'll assume you're at the adult evening program in the diningroom. If you decide to skip the program and take a walk -- <u>let the counselors know and then check back with them when you return.</u>

If you decide to remain in the cabin or room with your children when they go to bed, <u>just let the counselors know that they do not need to check your cabin.</u>

An adult should be back in each room or cabin by the end of Shmirah so that our counselors can get some sleep, too. <u>When you return to the cabin or room let the counselors know you're back.</u>

ALSO -- We've included some 'post-it' notes in your packet. Put one on the <u>outside</u> of your door when you're in for the night. The counselors will know that you are in and they will not open your door to check on your kid(s).

4. During the day, when it's time for the kids to go off in their groups with their counselors, kids and counselors will meet at the <u>end</u> of the <u>preceeding</u> activity -- which means: mornings <u>after tefilla,</u> afternoons at snack. Deliver your child to his or her counselor. Meet kids and counselors back at the diningroom at the time specified in the schedule.

The counselors have planned a full and varied program for their groups. Every group will have lots of time in the playground, sports and games, singing with Allison and Janet, crafts, dancing with Varda, movement with Dawn and daily study/discussion sessions on different Jewish topics.

Kids will not swim with their groups. (We have no lifeguard so swimming will be a family activity -- with your children under your own supervision.) If the weather is very hot we will add in some water-play activities to keep everyone cool.

It's critical to health, safety and peace of mind that we know where our children are and who is supervising them at all times. The counselors are directly responsible only during the times specified in the program. Which means, you are the 'supervisor' during all other times.) <u>If for any reason your child is not joining his/her group for a counselor led activity, please tell the counselor this yourself!!!</u>

5. The books in our book corner are here for you and your family to enjoy during the week. You can borrow them and take them to read in your cabin or outside in the sun. Just be sure to return them to the same table when you are finished with them. Any of these books which you'd like to buy for your family's library can be ordered by phone from Bob & Bob, the Jewish bookstore in Palo Alto. (The Storyteller in Lafayette and Cody's in Berkeley also have lots of Jewish books.)

6. All meals will be served buffet style. Please try to be on time so that we can start and end together. Lunch and dinner will end with a communal birkat hamazon (blessing after meals). We've left breakfast as a more open-ended meal in terms of timing.

As the kids finish eating there will be 2 counselors available in the diningroom who will read and organize quiet games which you can finish your meals and your conversations. When most people are finished we will call the kids back to the tables so we can say birkat hamazon together. Please don't give your kids permission to leave the diningroom.

Our kitchen is being run by Cherie B.   who is here with her daughter.

7. We've planned our tefilla (our prayer services) to be a joyful and family oriented experience. We hope you come, give it a try and join in even if ('organized') prayer is not one of your regular Jewish activities.

8. We look forward to celebrating a traditional Shabbat* together here at camp. Shabbat begins with candle-lighting at sunset and lasts until havdallah at sunset

---

* you'll be receiving a separate packet of Shabbat materials

the next night. In keeping with the experience we've tried to create, there will be no cooking done on Shabbat (everything we'll eat on Shabbat is either fresh or has been cooked before Shabbat and warmed in ovens which are pre-heated) and we've planned no crafts or writing activities to take place on Shabbat.

This will also explain why we will make two pots of coffee and two of hot water **before** Shabbat (and if we run out we will be unable to make more until Shabbat is over).

This Shabbat happens to be the very longest Shabbat of the year which is wonderful for us because we get to enjoy it together for that much longer. Sunset is actually not until about 8:00 pm although we will light candles and start our Shabbat earlier at about 6:15. We cannot make Havdallah (the ceremony marking the transition from Shabbat back to the weekday world until about 9:00 pm. (We can start Shabbat before sunset, making it longer, but we can't end it earlier than sunset.) We realize that this means that many of our younger campers may not be able to stay awake for havdallah. Perhaps with nice long Shabbat naps everyone will be able to make it!!!

9. In your packet, you received name-tags for each member of your family. Please wear one each day, at least until Shabbat. It helps us get to know each other and saves wear and tear on those of us who take longer to learn names!

10. We have been assured that prior to our arrival everything in camp is in good working condition -- however if a problem develops, please let us know. The camp does have a care-taker on the premises.

11. At the end of Shabbat Camp on Sunday, we will be setting up a Shabbat Camp Grocery Store at which we will be selling any leftover food (at great prices). This undertaking helps us balance our budget (a bit). Please look for the set up at lunch time on Sunday and help us out if you can. If we have anything leftover after that which can't be saved or used by our teenage retreat program, we will distribute it to the homeless.

12. If you should need to find them between midnight and early morning -- Vicky and Janet will both be sleeping in building #11 which is right next door to the diningroom.

p.s. Rules about using the boats: kids will not be boating with their groups. Boating is a family activity which means -- kids in boats **with** adults (no kids out alone). **All kids and non-swimmer adults must wear life jackets**. DO NOT USE THE KYACKS.

THE WEDNESDAY: Family Camper

get those pennies ready!!!

1. Please remember to send your Kochavim, Keshet, Shemesh camper with bathing suit, towel and sunscreen. Towel and bathing suit will remain up at bunk 1/2 to dry.

2. Haverim go boating at Lake Casitas today, departing at about 10:30 and returning at about 3:30. No one goes without hat and sunscreen.

3. Please move ALL cars to parking lot.

4. Canteen open 2-3. For sale: sundries and Ramah stuff.

5. Note today's "specials"
   - <u>Aerobics with Dawn</u> — 9:45-10:30 in the dining room (parents)
   - <u>Study with Eddy</u> — prepare for the high holidays with a guided tour of the machzor (the high holiday prayer book) 3:15-4:15 pm (bet knesset) (parents)
   - (family) bubble blowing 4:30 near meeting rock
   - <u>Singing for everyone</u> at 5:30 in the Bet Knesset.

6. Please continue to wear your name tags.

7. re: Shmira: please check OUT and IN with the counselors on Shmirah in your area so they know when your kids are "covered."

---

8. Thought for the day:

Joshua ben Perahyah taught: Select a master-teacher for yourself; Acquire a colleague* for study; When you assess people, tip the balance in their favor.	יְהוֹשֻׁעַ בֶּן־פְּרַחְיָה אוֹמֵר: עֲשֵׂה לְךָ רַב, וּקְנֵה לְךָ חָבֵר*, וֶהֱוֵי דָן אֶת־כָּל־הָאָדָם לְכַף זְכוּת.

*friend

---

9. Family Camp Quiz
   - 101 level: who are the siblings among our counselors?
   - 201 level: who are the siblings among our parents?

{ When you know the answer, tell Jessica (drama). Prize to 1st. }

THE Family Camper

PREP FOR

WEDNESDAY:

Please check your mailbox (in the lounge) before breakfast for the day's schedule, any messages, etc.

Keshet and Shemesh should <u>bring</u> bathingsuit and sunscreen rolled up in a towel WITH THEM TO BREAKFAST. (they will swim in the late morning; There <u>will be</u> a lifeguard present.)

Haverim will be going boating (row boats) at nearby Lake Casitas. Sunscreen and hats A MUST! (bring to breakfast)

- they'll be leaving at about 10:30 and will be back by 3:00. They're taking sack lunches from camp.
- Lake Casitas is about 7 miles from camp
- counselors will drive them there and be in boats with them
- this is a reservoir. (NO SWIMMING.)

Keep wearing your name tag, please!

THE SUNDAY Family Camper

last day

1. At breakfast - please say good-bye to: Jessica, Yitzchak and Chana, all of whom need to leave before lunch.
2. happy un-birthday to Felicia.
3. rosters* will be mailed to you within a few weeks
4. sandwiches will be ready today ~~sxh~~ when we finish our birthday party.
5. Please bring any "lost & found" items down to the office_____.
6. thought for the day:

> Jews have a job to do. We have to gather the sparks of God's light and do תִקוּן עוֹלָם/tikun olam, repair of the world.
>
> The Jew is supposed to be a fixer — God's partner in completing creation.

7. Something to talk about in the car on the way home: how can your family be God's partner in the coming new year?

have a great new year!
שָׁנָה טוֹבָה

[* of campers and staff]

Hand-outs 161

first day

21 August 1991 **WEDNESDAY** 11 Elul 5751

PARENTS	Keshet, Shemesh, Haverim	Yedidim
12:30 LUNCH		
1:30–2:15 !!HELLO FAMILY CAMP!! general orientation, singing, meet counselors and kids		
2:30–3:30 FAMILY SWIM *please note: we have no lifeguard for this swim – remember: YOU are (always) your child's lifeguard		
Snack		
4:00 walk Yedidim to Yellow building (the "Gan")	meet counselors at meeting rock	at the Gan
4:05 parents meeting [Bet Knesset/chapel] ALL QUESTIONS ANSWERED		
4:45–5:45 STUDY SESSIONS		
5:45 pick up Yedidim meet other kids at meeting rock	meet parents at meeting rock	pick up by parents
dancing & DINNER 6:15		
7–7:45 FAMILY EVENING PROGRAM		
	Kids 7 and under go with parents for bedtime, walks, stargazing, etc., laila tov! (goodnight) Shemesh & Haverim – stay: program until about 8:45 (counselors will walk them home)	

9:15 Shmira (babysitting begins)

9:30–10:30 parents pro evening program followed by snack and Israeli dancing

11:30 Shmira ends (A parent must be back in each room, bunk, tent by 11:30 so our counselors can sleep, too. when you go back – check in with the counselors (so they know the kids are covered)

1991

the NEW Friday schedule
Erev Shabbat • almost Shabbat

Action Notes:

welcome Paul Gee! (who arrived yesterday afternoon)

welcome our Shabbat guests: Jerry Gelbart, Rabbi Stuart Kelman, Paul Weiss

Shabbat Shalom!

Planning Notes:

1. 8-8:45 breakfast
2. 9-9:30 tefilla
3. Family Challah making in the dining room — every family will make a challah
6. 10:15 - 12:15 | 10:15 - 11:00
7. [Kids] meet counsellors | [parents] free time; pool open
8. group time | discussion with Vicky; Shabbat 101 - bring your questions: both practical and profound
11. 11:15 study session with JODY
12. 12:15 lunch
13. 1-3 rest time
14. open arts & crafts: meet Annette for a new art experience!!
16. 3-4:15 | 3-4:15
17. [Kids] Group time | [parents] discussion with Vicky: Talking About the "G-word" (God) with Kids
20. 4:15 family time • pool open 'til 5:15
21. shower/dress for Shabbat (nbe) / wear white if you have it!
22. 6:15 candle lighting - dining room - bring your candleholders
23. Kabbalat Shabbat - welcoming Shabbat. (Kiva)
24. 7:00 Shabbat dinner
25. Family Oneg Shabbat (Shabbat Celebration)
27. 9:15 shmira
28. 9:30 parents Oneg Shabbat; featuring BRAD BURSTON who will answer the question: "Why would a (seemingly) sane person like you choose to live in as (seemingly) crazy a place as Israel?" and other questions you might have about life in "the middle east."
31. 11:00 laila tov!

Counselors' version of the new FRIDAY morning schedule

1. 8: – 8:45 bkfst
2. 9 – 9:30 tefilla
3. family challah baking until 10:15   HELP!
5. 10:15 – 12:15
6. kids in groups   parents ~~free time & study~~
7. 10:15 – 10:30 meet and circle time

	10:30 – 10:50	10:55 – 11:15	11:20 – 11:40	11:45 – 12:05
☆☆	dancing with Varda	carrot seed activity	Annette get ready for shabbat project	singing with Allison
♀♀	singing with Allison	dancing with Varda	bowling	Annette shabbat art project
~~	games, bowling	singing with Allison	dancing with Varda	bake brownies and set lunch tables

meet Annette in art room; meet Allison where you met her yesterday ~~(near fountain;)~~ meet Varda in kiva

12:15 lunch
1 – 3:00 rest   COUNSELORS' MEETING AT 1:00

3 – 4:15
  kids in groups
  ☆☆☆ art project (salt & chalk) / baseball / spice box
  ♀♀ moon art project ~~and~~ playground / spice box
  ~~~ meet Annette in art room / story

4:15 – 6:15 family time · pool time · shower time · get ready for shabbat time!

6:15 ⎫ candle lighting
7:00 ⎭ Kabbalat Shabbat
7:00 dinner   שבת
7:15 – 8:00 oneg shabbat   ! שלום !
9:30 shmira
    adult evening program
    |
11:00 laila tov!

EREV SHABBAT (FRI)

PARENTS		Yedidim
BREAKFAST		
8:45 → the GREAT FAMILY CAMP HALLAH BAKE OFF EVENT!		
9:30 → TEFILLAH		
10:00 → 10-11 free time / pool open	meeting rock / Kids' group time	walk kids to Yedidim
		pick up at Gan
12:45 meet kids / dancing and lunch	meeting rock	
1:30 REST TIME ★ for "nonresting" families: ART STUFF with Chana — FINISH YOUR MASK OR SOMETHING NEW OR help us count our pennies - IN THE NEW LIBRARY		
3:00		
3:15 / 4:15 PARENTS' pre-shabbat stuff:	meeting rock	to Gan
☆ experience God in the natural world - meet Mitch at rock	Group time - groups get ready for Shabbat	
☆ Improvise - the new library (Jessica)		
☆ talk - Shabbat 101 - getting ready/Shabbat going in your family - PAM in the "old library"		
(Buy your Shabbatagrams!) Shabbat 201 - keeping Shabbat going in a family - VICKY in the lounge		
4:30 snack	meeting rock	pick up at Gan
ORIGAMI for SHABBAT with JON - meet in the old library (4:30-5:15)		
pool 4:45-5:15		
5:30 GET READY - SHABBAT IS ALMOST HERE		
Shower, bubble bath, do laundry, contemplate your soul ETC		
6:00 candlelighting in dining room		
6:15 KABBALAT SHABBAT	✲ שבת שלום! ✲	
6:45 Shabbat dinner		
7:30 - 8:15 ONEG SHABBAT		

	Keshet and Yedidim - laila tov
9 PM - Shmira begins	Shemesh and Haverim - ONEG
9:30 - Shack	SHABBAT (til 9-ish)
parents evening program: A CHANCE TO TALK ABOUT JEWISH FAMILY STUFF	
11 pm - Shmira ENDS	

1991

THURSDAY
23 August 1991 — 12 Elul 1991

	PARENTS	Keshet Shemesh Haverim	Yedidim
8:00 →	BREAKFAST		
8:45 →	TEFILLA – Bet Knesset (Chapel)		
9:30 →	free time — courts, pool, fields available [10:00 "baby drop-off" in new library] 11–12:30 study sessions	meet at meeting rock Kids study sessions and activities with Counselors 10:30 Haverim out to Lake Casitas back by 2:30	drop off at Gan
12:30	special singing with Allison (bet Knesset)	12:45 meeting rock	pick up at Gan
1:00 →	dancing and lunch		
1:30	REST TIME	* for "non-resting" families: ART STUFF with Chana (go to art room – building above pool a) play tennis, frisbee, etc. read a book, have a conversation...	
3:00	free time: pool open, etc., discussion with Vicky: "Parents as Resident theologians" (lounge)	meeting rock Kids' group time meeting rock	drop off at Gan pick up at Gan
4:30 →	SNACK FAMILY TIME FAMILY SWIM OR FAMILY DANCING (w/ Goel; you know where) OR FAMILY OUTDOOR ADVENTURE WITH MITCH (meet at meeting rock)		
5:30	Singing with Allison (in the Bet Knesset) dancing & DINNER (6:15)		
7:00 –	FAMILY Evening program followed by an all camp bedtime story time		
	shmira begins at 9:15 parents evening program 9:30–11:00 Snack dancing with Goel "fun and games" PLEASE "CHECK IN" with the counselor when you get back 11:30 laila tov!	Yedidim and Keshet with parents laila tov! (good night) halomot paz (sweet dreams) Shemesh and Haverim – remain... will be accompanied "home" at program's end	

שַׁבָּת
SHABBAT!

PARENTS	KESHET	SHEMESH	HAVERIM	YEDIDIM / KOCHAVIM ✶★✦

8:30 → ✸ SHABBAT SHALOM! — **BREAKFAST** — שבת שלום! ✸
9:15 → **TEFILLAH**

9:45 — Leave with their counselors for their own tefillot and other Shabbat stuff.

parents walk Yedidim-to Gan, Kochavim-to Moadon Kochavim

KIDDISH

11:00 → to 12:30(ish)
POOL OPEN (shared with older kids and counselors)

☆☆ Deborah Lipstadt: The "Yes-But" Syndrome — denying the holocaust.

☆ Meeting Rock

PICK UP AT GAN / MOADON KOCHAVIM

12:45
LUNCH!
1:30 →

MENUCHA - rest Shabbat Family Time : Naps

POOL OPENS at 2:00 (til 4:30) walk, talk, play ball, etc.,
2:00 "REAL BASKETBALL"

4:00 Snack

4:45 Family Bubble Blowing near meeting rock
led by Donna & Maya L

5:30 for Keshet, their parents and everyone else who enjoys a great show:
the Keshet theatre festival - in the new library

6:15 SE'UDAH SHLISHEET • The 3rd Shabbat Meal
SHABBAT FUN

8:00 HAVDALLAH Shavua tov! שבוע טוב! have a good week!

LAILA TOV! YEDIDIM & KESHET !!
Sweet dreams!!

9 PM - SHEMESH & HAVERIM & PARENTS and any other family members who are awake! — GET READY FOR THE NEW YEAR - a special family activity — dining room

9:15 SHMIRA (until 12:00)
10:30 - Family Slichot* services
-11:00
11-12 parents' program
12 pm Shmira ends.

* Special Rosh Hashana "warm up" prayers, usually said at midnight the Saturday night before Rosh Hashana.

THE Family Camp er

thursday morning 23 Aug 1991 IZEUL

1. Today's the day we're combining our PENNIES. If you forgot to bring yours to breakfast, you can bring them to lunch. Watch them add up.

2. Remember Shemesh & Keshet bring sunscreen and bathing suits rolled in towel with them this morning.

3. Haverim – off to rowboating at Casitas. Leaving at 11ish. Back by 2:30ish. <u>No one goes without hat and sunscreen.</u> Any questions – ask Sacha or Marc.

4. note today's "specials"
   - ART STUFF for the FAMILY / for "non-resting" family members; art room during resttime (1:45-2:45)
   - discussion (for interested parents) with Vicky: "Parents as resident theologians: talking about God with kids" during your afternoon free time (3:30 in lounge)
   - Singing with Allison at end of afternoon (5:30 in Bet Knesset)

5. today's FAMILY CAMP QUIZ
   level 1: How many water fountains are there at Camp Ramah?
   level 2: How many <u>Biblical</u> names do we have here among our campers?
   submit answers to Jordan by dinner-time

6. thought for today:

   ✱ All the wide world is beautiful, and it matters but little where we go.... The spot where we chance to be always seems the best.
   (John Muir)

THE Family Camper
FRI ♥LUNCHTIME♥

more stuff:

1. 1:45-3 during Rest Time:
   (1) open art room for families
   * If you have a mask to finish — SCOOT UP THERE IMMEDIATELY AND GET TO WORK
   * If you want to come start something new — plan to arrive at about 2:15

   (2) Volunteer to help us count our pennies!!!
   Come to the new library at 2:00

2. WE MUST HAVE sign-ups for our Sunday morning boating adventure... (People under 14 can fish — without a license. Over 14: $8.50.) Sign up before 4:30

   also — aliyah and Torah reading signups

3. Canteen open 2-3
   ramah paraphenalia & toiletries

4. remember: Parents Shabbat prep:
   3:15 — ★ Experience God in the natural world — meet Mitch at rock
   4:15   ★ improvise — in the new library with Jessica
          ★ Shabbat 101 ... getting Shabbat going in your family
             Pam — in the "old library"
          ★ Shabbat 201 ... keeping Shabbat going in a family —
             Vicky — in the lounge

THE Family Camper

Thursday
1 September 1988
19 Elul 5748

1. Janet Harris feels that the morning is too long for some of our littlest yeddidim. We would like to try a shorter morning so please bring your two and three year olds to the Gan at 10:00 AM. Here's to our happy campers!

2. Yashar Ko-ach to Shoshana Rose on the occasion of her first jump off the high dive. She's been preparing since last family camp and came back ready to do it!

3. Back by popular demand: Dawn M leading Aerobics starting 15 minutes after tefilla this morning AND Friday morning.

4. Shelly Dorph's study group: Confronting Your Personal Theology will continue today from 3-4:30 in the Bet Knesset (chapel).

5. We are looking for Torah readers for Shabbat morning (for aliyot of a few verses) if you're interested see Stu Kelman THIS MORNING.

6. Look in your box at lunch for further details about the fishing trip.

7. Julie W (of shemesh) has volunteered to be the official family camp journal writer. Todah Rabbah!

8. There don't seem to be enough golfers here at family camp to organize a formal outing but if people want to go as individuals we'll help you.

9. And the winner is: MARY HAD A LITTLE LAMB! (Ba Ba)

10. Maariv services will begin in the chapel immediately after Rad Hayom.

11. We assume you are still working on yesterday's quiz question... try these:

Family camp Quiz:
1. Can you name 2 of the 3 pairs of sisters among our counselors.
2. What do a rainbow 🌈 and a slice of bread 🍞 have in common?

Leave your answers in Vicky's box.

THE Family Camp er

LUNCHTIME EDITION
~~Tuesday~~ Wednesday 31 August
18 Elul

1. Happy Un-Birthday Jenny F
2. Thanks DAWN for the aerobics — we'll make it a daily event.
3. HERE'S THE MISSING INFORMATION FROM TODAY'S SCHEDULE:
    3-4:30   Parents: POOL, TENNIS, ETC
        Shelly's study session: Confronting Your Personal Theology
            place changed TO Bet K'nesset
        Keshet, Shemesh, Haverim - with counselors
                rendez-vous at meeting rock
        Yedidim - at the Gan
    4:30 your choice: FAMILY SWIM or FAMILY NATURE HIKE (meet at meeting rock)
    5:30 in Bet K'nesset: SINGING WITH Allison!
4. parents of ☀️ and 👫: leave out bathing suits and leave kids' room unlocked am & pm
5. WINNER OF FAMILY QUIZ #1: Josh h!
    get the # and locations from him!
    (there's an old Ramah legend that: If you drink from each fountain while you're here, good luck will come to you in the New Year [it rhymes, too]).
6. re: S'HMIRA: check out <u>and in</u> with the counselors. If you're staying <u>in</u>... let counselor know that, too!
7. FAMILY CAMP QUIZ #2
    1. How many <u>Ariels</u> are there in camp?
    2. How many <u>Elanas</u> (or <u>Ilanas</u>) are there in camp?
    3. How many <u>former</u> Ramah directors are there in camp?
PUT YOUR ANSWERS, IN WRITING, IN VICKY'S BOX IN THE LOUNGE
& DON'T FORGET TO SIGN YOUR NAME!
8. HAVE FUN!

Shabbat

The problem with the usual definition of Shabbat as a day of rest is the meaning of the word "rest." (And because it's hard to define "rest" without also defining its opposite, part of the problem is also defining the word "work.")

In **everyday** speech, "work" usually means job, expending energy to produce or accomplish something, implying an end product. "Rest" is usually used to mean a relaxing non-job activity which has enjoyment as its end goal.

These definitions do fit **everyday** speech ... but because Jewish time is divided into **everyday** and the **seventh day** (Shabbat) ... we need to find an additional definition for these words—one which fits the **seventh day**.

Two well known Jewish thinkers, Abraham Joshua Heschel and Eric Fromm have provided **seventh day** definitions of "work" and "rest" which shed light on the concept of Shabbat as a day of rest.

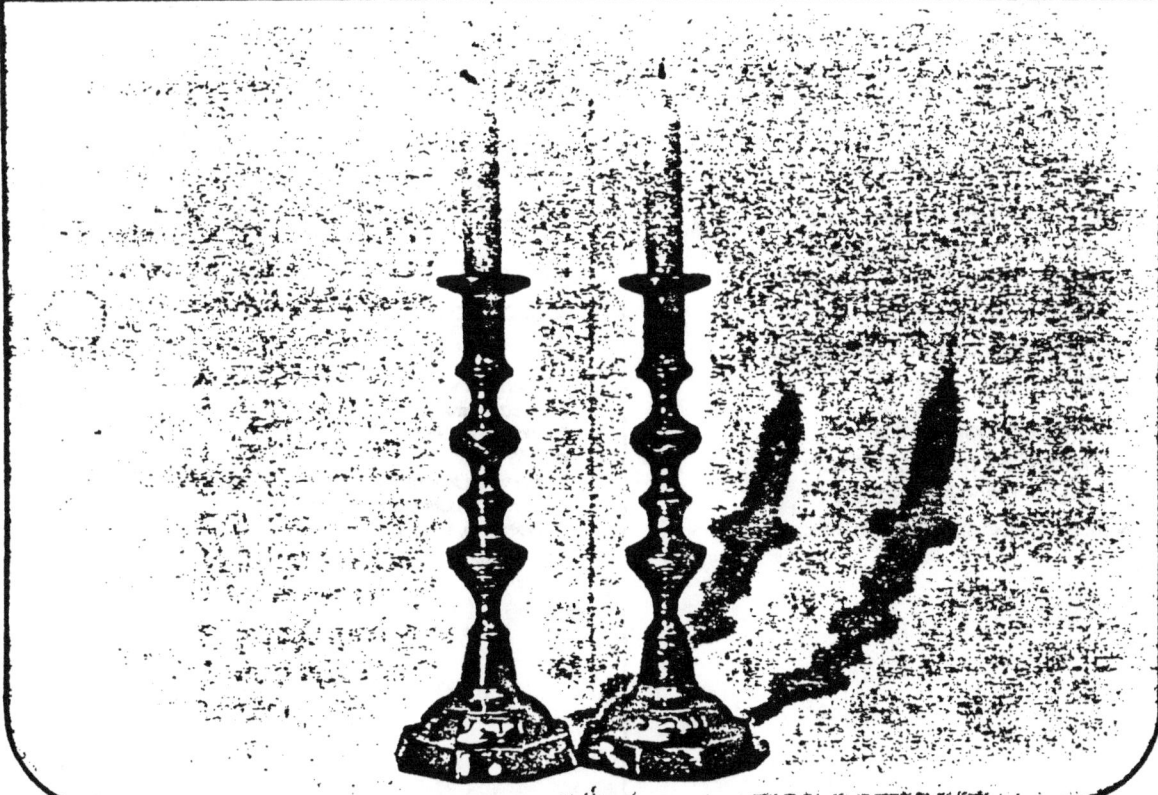

Eric Fromm said:

Work is any interference with the physical world or any kind of disturbance in the natural or social equilibrium of the world; (This would include physical labor as would our '**everyday**' definition of work, but it would also include picking a flower or lighting a match, arranging a legal transaction or buying something).

Rest is a state of peace between human life and the natural world; complete harmony between people and between people and nature; Non-participation in any process of change.

Shabbat is a day of rest; an experience of complete harmony with the world.[1]

Abraham Joshua Heschel said:

Work is involvement in technology; concern with the technical and spatial side of civilization; energy directed toward subduing, managing and controlling the forces of nature.

Rest is independence from technology; a turning to concern with the non-tangible aspects of civilization specifically with time; the only energy expended is toward the inner self, toward establishing the human as sovereign over technology;

Shabbat is a day of rest; an armistice in the struggle for existence; an island of stillness in time.[2]

These **seventh day** definitions of work and rest are crucial to the concept of Shabbat as a day of rest. Working is clearly not the equivalent of physical labor while rest is its absence. Neither is rest a labor-saving measure. Shabbat rest makes a statement about human beings and the universe: Even though people must work, work is not the **goal** of human existence. It also makes a statement about the quality of life. Meaningful living is not built of things—but of intangibles: values, relationships and time.

The Shabbat rituals—candles, kiddush and hallot, special clothes, time spent in the synagogue, time with friends and family, havdalah—are the tools we use to create our day of rest, to frame the **seventh day** and to set it off from the **everyday**.[2]

1. Erich Fromm, You Shall Be As Gods, (A Fawcett Premier Book), Fawcett Publications, Greenwich CT, 1969, pp.152-157
2. Abraham Joshua Heschel, The Sabbath, The Jewish Publication Society, Philadelphia, 1963, pp.13-24

36

Together: #3
The Melton Research Center, NYC
Vicky Kelman

Here at Ramah, this understanding of שבת [Shabbat] translates into the following kinds of guidelines in terms of our community observence of שבת [Shabbat]:

There is no driving in or out of around camp.

The laundry is closed

No food is cooked on שבת [Shabbat]...the food we eat has all been prepared in advance and is only warmed.

None of our programs utilize writing, drawing, coloring or other crafts.

The office is closed.

The pool and sports facilities are open, as on the schedule.

It's a great day for hikes, walks reading and conversation.

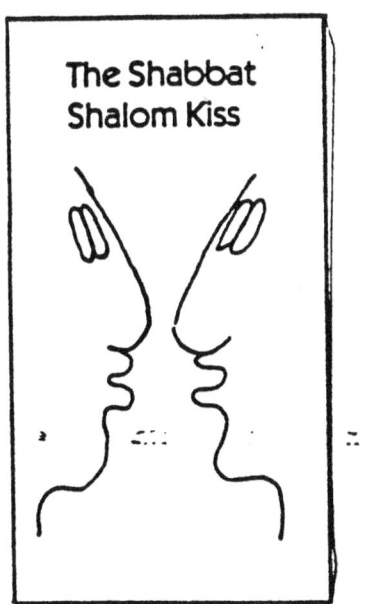

The Shabbat Shalom Kiss

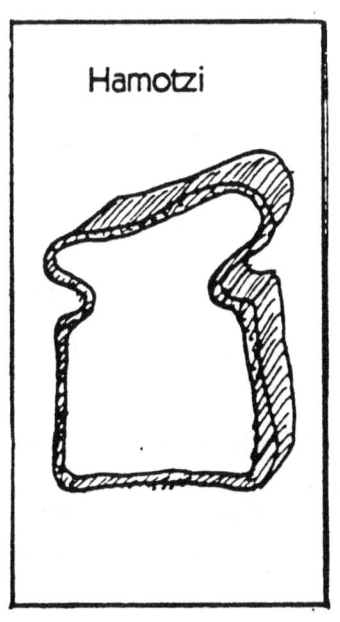

Hamotzi

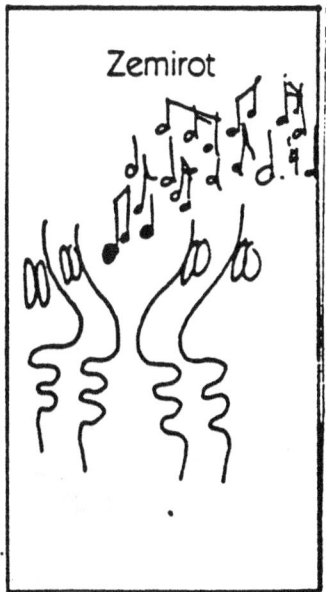

Zemirot

שבת SHABBAT!

PARENTS	KESHET	SHEMESH	HAVERIM	YEDIDIM

8:30 → SHABBAT SHALOM! | BREAKFAST | שבת שלום!

9:15 → TEFILLA

9:45 Keshet & Shemesh leave with their counselors for their own tefillot and other "Shabbat stuff" — haverim, too! | parents walk yedidim to Gan

KIDDUSH

11:00 to 12:30(ish)
POOL OPEN
(shared with older kids and counselors)

study: Bedtime, Birthday parties & Blessings: Ritual in family life (with Vicky)

MEETING ROCK | PICKUP AT GAN

12:45 LUNCH

1:30 MENUCHA – rest   SHABBAT FAMILY TIME: NAPS
POOL OPENS at 2:00 (til 4:30) walk, talk, play ball, etc.,
4:00 snack
4:-4:45 Family Bubble Blowing – meet Elana and Marc near meeting rock
4:45 Shemesh & Haverim – meet Jessica at amphitheatre
5:15–6:00 THE FAMILY CAMP SHABBAT THEATER FESTIVAL

6:15 SE'UDAH SHLISHEET • The 3rd Shabbat meal
↓
SHABBAT FUN
↓
8:00 HAVDALLAH Shavua tov! = שבוע טוב! = have a good week!

LAILA TOV Yedidim and Keshet!!
Sweet dreams!

SHEMESH & HAVERIM
'til 8:45 (ish) – night hike with Mitch flashlights!!

9:15 SHMIRA (until 11:30)
9:30 SNACK IN LOUNGE
Parents' evening program

Ready! Set! Go!

Preparing to Celebrate Rosh HaShana

Tonight's evening a program will help us get ready for Rosh HaShana. Everyone in camp is invited.

part 1: **Ready!**   (8:30 to 9:30)   <u>in the evening program room</u>

Create a Rosh HaShana card for someone who's here at Family Camp.

Learn what an acrostic is and create one of your own!

Learn what teshuva is and how to do it.

Listen to the sounds of the Shofar -- a Jewish alarm clock! (Everyone can have a turn to blow, too.)

Sing Rosh HaShana melody with Uncle Shelly!

Part 2: **Set!**   (9:30 - 10:30)   <u>in the dining room</u>

<u>Hand-made Midrash:</u>
     The first chapters of Genesis talk about God, Human Beings, the world and their relationships to one another. These are some of the same themes that Rosh HaShana is about.
     Tonight we will try to connect ourselves to these elements in Rosh HaShana using the texts we've all been studying. Working with paper and glue we will explore our personal connections to these themes.

Part 3: **Go!**   (10:30 - 11:00-ish)   <u>in the Bet K'nesset</u>

<u>Selichot:</u>
     The Saturday night before Rosh HaShana we come together as a community to recite special prayers.

☐ TAKE A LONG SHABBAT NAP AND COME WITH YOUR WHOLE FAMILY!!!!!!☐

"Which is greater, the works of man or of God?" the pagan Tineus Rufus asked. Rabbi Akiba replied that the works of man are greater than those of God, and illustrated his contention by presenting Tineus Rufus with sheaves of wheat and loaves of cake. The cakes are greater; not that the works of God are less worthy, but that the full measure of divinity is expressed through the interaction between God's nature and humankind, the crown of His creation. The *Motzi* prayer is not recited over sheaves of wheat nor is the *Kiddush* recited over clusters of grapes. The *Motzi* is recited over the bread that is made through human effort and the *Kiddush* is recited over the fruit of the vine that human ingenuity cultivates. Both benedictions exemplify the power and goodness of God—as expressed through the works of human beings.

1.

At home I was taught that if a piece of bread falls from the table, it should quickly be picked up and *kissed*: Bread is God's gift. Once, around the third meal of the Sabbath, so I was told and taught, the disciples of the Rebbe persisted in asking him to tell them where God is. He remained silent, but at last recited the *Motzi*, the blessing over the bread, and pointed to the loaf of bread on the table.

2.

A Kiss Before Reading

Salman Rushdie.

I grew up kissing books and bread.

In our house, whenever anyone dropped a book or let fall a chapati or a "slice," which was our word for a triangle of buttered leavened bread, the fallen object was required not only to be picked up but also kissed, by way of apology for the act of clumsy disrespect. I was as careless and butterfingered as any child and, accordingly, during my childhood years, I kissed a large number of "slices" and also my fair share of books.

Devout households in India often contained, and still contain, persons in the habit of kissing holy books. But we kissed everything. We kissed dictionaries and atlases. We kissed Enid Blyton novels and Superman comics. If I'd ever dropped the telephone directory I'd probably have kissed that, too.

All this happened before I had ever kissed a girl. In fact it would almost be true, true enough for a fiction writer, anyhow, to say that once I started kissing girls, my activities with regard to bread and books lost some of their special excitement. But one never forgets one's first loves.

Bread and books: food for the body and food for the soul — what could be more worthy of our respect, and even love?

It has always been a shock to me to meet people for whom books simply do not matter.   *From "Imaginary Homelands."*

3.

1.&2. H. Shulweis, Moment Magazine, vol 10, #4, April 1985
3. Salman Rushdie, New York Times Book Review; "Noted with pleasure" column; p. 1992

directions

Some of our thinking and learning here at family camp has been getting us ready for the start of a new year. Some of the traditional things to think about at this season are hopes, wishes, and plans for our family in the new year.

We are asking every Family Camp family to spend a few minutes between now and the beginning of Shabbat writing a letter to yourselves which includes your plans, hopes and wishes for your family in the new year (feel free to illustrate).

Put your finished letter in the envelope, seal and address it to your family at home. Bring your letter to candle lighting tonight. We will mail it to you. Enjoy!

A LETTER TO OUR family FROM OUR family

ROSH HASHANAH
1 TISHREI 5749

Family Stuff

1. Something our family loves to do together is _____

2. One of our happiest moments as a family was _____

3. A Jewish decision our family has made _____

4. Some religious differences between my family now and the family I grew up in are _____

5. My current plans for my kids' Jewish education are _____

6. A Jewish wish I have for my family is _____

7. A Jewish parenting question I've always wanted to ask another family is _____

Netivot Shalom Shabbaton

BINGO

Find Someone Who

Has a Teddy Bear.	Was born in the same month as you.	Has built a Sukkah.	Has taken ballet lessons.	Is a Giants fan.
Thinks chocolate is the solution to all problems.	Likes to read science fiction.	Does not like scary movies.	Plays a musical instrument.	Is a gourmet cook.
Has a relative who is/was a rabbi.	Has planted a tree.	Is/was a student at UC Berkeley or Berkeley High.	Born in Chicago, Libya, or Israel.	Attends poetry readings.
Lived in California as a child.	Is/was a member of a Jewish Youth Group.	Is/was the president of something.	Goes bowling or folk dancing on Wednesday nights.	Is not left handed.
Bakes their own challah or hamentaschen.	Is left handed.	Is a fan of George Burns & Gracie Allen.	Likes to do photography.	Has a pet with an Aramaic, Hebrew, or Jewish name.

and write that person's name in the correct box

Congregation Netivot Shalom
Berkeley CA
(Claire Sherman)

1. Much religious education is already happening in families; it simply has not been named. The parent who responds to a baby's cry has already taught that child the first and most important lesson on prayer: when you cry out at night, someone answers. The kindergartener who is lovingly prepared for the first day of school knows all about the God who prepares a way in the wilderness.

2. In most crisis situations, such as an earthquake, flood, or fire, parents instinctively reach out and grab hold of their children, bringing them to safety first. In the crisis of divorce, however, mothers and fathers put children on hold, attending to adult problems first. Divorce is associated with a diminished capacity to parent in almost all dimensions — discipline, playtime, physical care, and emotional support. Divorcing parents spend less time with their children and are less sensitive to their children's needs. At this time they may very well confuse their own needs with those of their children.

3. Parents need to realize that all religious training cannot be carried out in institutional situations. Combining class hours and homework hours, children are exposed to general education well over 1,000 hours a year. In comparison, they have institutional religious training usually less than 100 hours a year.

4. Divorce is much more than the coup de grâce of a stressful marriage. It is a new beginning that offers people second chances. It is no more and no less than an opportunity to rebuild lives. And there's

5. It has long been known that the family has the strongest, most intense effect on individuals in their development; but the concept of the family, as a system in need of care and nurture, is a new notion in our society. If we expect individuals within the family to give and to receive love and acceptance, we must see that the family, as a complete unit, receives warmth and support.

Shabbat Camp
June 1990
A.J.E.

6. The challenge for us is to help parents create practices that will nourish as well as define the family. We know that rituals give us a sense of belonging to a larger community. Steven Wolin and Linda Bennett conclude in a study (George Washington University Center for Family Research) that ritual life is important, because it reinforces the family's identity and gives all members a shared and necessary sense of belonging.[6] Ritual provides us with strength in times of trouble, meaning in times of chaos, closeness in times of joy. "All families need rituals to survive. Rituals are a boundary. They say when you are in and when you are out. And when you are inside the family you feel better"[7] (Wolin and Bennett). The pursuit of meaningful rituals takes time and commitment. Such efforts will bring their own rewards

7. Divorce is also the only major family crisis in which social supports fall away. When there is a death in the family, people come running to help. After a natural disaster, neighbors rally to assist those who have been hurt. After most such crises, clergymen may call on the family to console adults or speak with children who are badly shaken. But not so with divorce. Friends are afraid that they will have to take sides; neighbors think it is none of their business. Although half the families in our study belong to churches or synagogues, not one clergyman came to call on the adults or children during divorce. Grandparents may be helpful but are apprehensive about getting caught in the crossfire. They often live far away and feel their role is limited. When a man and a woman divorce, many people tend to act as if they believe it might be contagious.

8. To carry a child in this threatening world takes faith,
to give birth to a child in this frightening world takes love,
To raise a child to be a Jew takes courage.

9. Joseph Campbell, in a recent interview on PBS, asks, "Will our children have a spiritual life?" He answers his own question in much the same way that John Westerhoff answers the question, "Will our children have faith?" when he says, "Yes, if we cultivate a spiritual life for ourselves."

10. Few adults anticipate accurately what lies ahead when they decide to divorce. Life is almost always more arduous and more complicated than they expect. It is often more depleting and more lonely for at least one member of the marriage.

> Version #2
> these three paragraphs are substituted for their counterparts in version #1

4.   South African diamond miners spend their working lives sifting through thousands of tons of rock and dirt looking for a few tiny diamonds. Too often we tend to do just the opposite. We sift through the diamonds, eagerly searching for dirt. . . . Strong families are diamond experts:

6.   The challenge for us is to help parents create practices that will nourish as well as define the family. We know that rituals give us a sense of belonging to a larger community. Steven Wolin and Linda Bennett conclude in a study (George Washington University Center for Family Research) that ritual life is important, because it reinforces the family's identity and gives all members a shared and necessary sense of belonging.[6] Ritual provides us with strength in times of trouble, meaning in times of chaos, closeness in times of joy. "All families need rituals to survive. Rituals are a boundary. They say when you are in and when you are out. And when you are inside the family you feel better"[7] (Wolin and Bennett). The pursuit of meaningful rituals takes time and commitment. Such efforts will bring their own rewards

10.   "The most recent conversation in our house has been about our television watching habits. We — as a family — are evaluating how much we watch and what we watch. If a half-minute commercial can convince us to buy a certain toothpaste or cereal, doesn't it seem logical that a whole show can convince us to buy certain habits? We don't condone excessive drinking, marital infidelity, casual premarital sex, smoking, or violence. What influence does it have on our lives to watch all that on TV?

Paragraphs: a Family Talk Activity
Footnotes:

1. Kathy Chesto, Family Intergenerational Religious Education: The Director's Guide. (Kansas City, KS: Sheed and Ward, 198), p. 2.

2. Judith S. Wallerstein and Sandra Blakeslee, Second Chances: Men, Women and Children a Decade after Divorce (New York: Ticknor and Fields, 1989), p. 7

3. Delia Halverson, "Faithbuilding Lifestyles: Enabling Teachers and Parents to share their Faith with Children and Youth," Religious Education 83, no, 4 (Fall 1988), p. 527

4. Wallerstein, p. 7

5. Margaret Sawin, Family Enrichment with Family Clusters (Valley Forge, PA: Judson Press, 1979) p. 15

6. Roberta Nelson, "Parents as Resident Theologians," Religious Education 83, no.4 (fall 1988), p. 493

7. Wallerstein, p. 4

8. Ruth Brin, Harvest: Collected Poems and Prayers (New York, NY: The Reconstructionist Press, 1986), p. 129

9. Roberta Nelson, p. 493

10. Wallerstein, p. 4

version #2:

4. Nicholas Stinnett and J. deFrain, Secrets of Strong Families

6. Roberta K. Nelson, p. 293

10.

THE GENERATIONS

In a house which becomes a home,
one hands down and another takes up
the heritage of mind and hand,
laughter and tears, musings and deeds.

Love, like a carefully loaded ship,
crosses the gulf between generations.

Thus have ceremonies of passage:

> when you wed,
> when you are delivered of a child,
> and when you die;
> when you depart and when you return;
> when you plant and when you harvest.

Bring up your children.
It is not the function of some official
to hand them their inheritance.
If others impart to your children
your knowledge and your ideas,
they will lose all of you
that is wordless and full of wonder.

Build memories in your children,
lest they drag out their lives joylessly
in a land which seems an empty camping place;
lest they allow treasures to rot away
because they have not been given the keys.

We live not by things,
but by the meaning of things.
It is needful to transmit the passwords
from generation to generation.

Adapted from *The Wisdom of the Sands*[1]
by Antoine de St. Exupery
© 1950, 1978 by Harcourt, Brace and
Jovanovich

Lost in the Forest

Once our master, Rabbi Hayyim of Zans, told us this parable:

A man had been wandering about in a forest for several days unable to find the way out. Finally he saw a man approaching him in the distance. His heart was filled with joy. "Now I shall surely find out which is the right way out of this forest," he thought to himself. When they neared each other, he asked the man, "Brother, will you please tell me the way out of the forest? I have been wandering about in here for several days and I am unable to find my way out."

Said the other to him, "Brother, I do not know the way out either, for I too have been wandering about in here for many days. But this much I can tell you. Do not go the way that I have gone, for I know that it is not the way. Now come, let us search for the way out together."

Our master added: So it is with us. The one thing that each one of us knows is that the way we have been going until now is not the way. Now come, let us join hands and look for the way together."

this version taken from New Prayers for the High Holy Days edited by Rabbi Jack Riemer 1970, Media Judaica

GOOD CLEAN FUN

Bubble Solution Formula

⅔ cup *Dawn* liquid dishwashing detergent

add water to make one gallon

For tougher, longer lasting bubbles, add 1 tablespoon glycerine (available at your local drugstore)

We have found that the solution becomes better with age, and recommend that it be allowed to sit in an open container for at least one day before use.

If you are looking for interesting things to use for making bubbles, try hoops of any size, two drinking straws with string threaded through them, using the straws as handles, juice cans with the ends removed and taped together to make long trumpets, coat hanger shapes, Slinkys, even a circle made by your fingers. Let your imagination run wild.

THE EXPLORATORIUM

The Great SHABBAT Camp Alef-Bet Nature Hike

LOOK FOR THINGS THAT LOOK LIKE LETTERS OF THE HEBREW ALPHABET. Can You Find 5?

ק Kuf (k)	נ nun (n)	י yud (y)	ה hey (h)	א alef (silent)
ר resh (r)	ס samekh (s)	כ Kaf (k)	ו vav (v)	🍃
ש shin (sh)	ע ayin (silent)	🌳	ז zayin (z)	ב bet (b)
🍁	פ pay (p)	ל lamed (l)	ח het (ch)	ג gimmel (g)
ת taf (t)	צ tzadi (tz)	מ mem (m)	ט tet (t)	ד daled (d)

The Great SHABBAT CAMP Alef-Bet Nature Hike

THE GREAT SHABBAT CAMP SCAVENGER HUNT

FIND AND COLLECT

1. A family of leaves.
2. A twig that looks like something Jewish.
3. A bright flower.
4. A pet rock.
5. A pinecone or an acorn.
6. Five blades of grass.
7. Two sounds that you heard on your hike.
8. Something that smells sweet.
9. A leaf that has three colors or more.
10. A thought (to share with your family).

The Shabbat Camp Sunday morning Rock and Stroll

Stroll around camp with your family. Look for some rocks to make friends with. Find one for each family member. The one you choose should be at least the size of two fingers but not bigger than your fist.

Sit down together knee-to-knee.

1. LOOK at your rock: how many colors can you see on its surface?

2. FEEL your rock: close your eyes and use your hands --- find sharp places and smooth places. Is it heavy or light? Put it against your cheek -- how does it feel? Is it warm or cold?

3. SMELL your rock.

4. TASTE your rock -- well-- DON'T taste it but imagine what it would taste like to lick it...to munch it...

5. LISTEN to your rock and see what it has to tell you about its life as a rock. Was it always where you found it? Has it made a journey? Does it like living here at Shabbat camp? Tap it with your fingernail. What sound does it make?

6. Imagine getting smaller and smaller and smaller until you are so tiny that you can pretend that the rock is a small planet and you are exploring its surface. Can you imagine going inside? Tell a story about your journey.

7. Put your rocks in the middle between you. Close your eyes...feel all the rocks until you find yours (with your eyes closed).

When you're re-united with your own rock -- meet us back near the diningroom where you can add eyes, decorations and tails (if your wish) to make your rock into a Shabbat Camp pet rock to take home.

Be ready to introduce your family's new 'pets' to the rest of the Shabbat Camp families.

Martin Buber wrote: "When a person is singing and cannot carry the tune, and someone comes along who can carry the tune and joins the first person and sings along, the first person will be able to keep the tune, too. That is the secret of the bond between spirits." (Ten Rungs, p.85)

△ Write one way someone in your family helped you.

△ Write one way you helped someone in your family.

> A young man was asked by the Gerer Rabbi if he had learned Torah. "Just a little," replied the youth.
> "That is all anyone ever has learned of the Torah," was the Rabbi's answer.
> (Newman, The Hasidic Anthology, p. 478)

△ Write down some Torah that you know.

> א מֹשֶׁה קִבֵּל תּוֹרָה מִסִּינַי,
> וּמְסָרָהּ לִיהוֹשֻׁעַ, וִיהוֹשֻׁעַ לִזְקֵנִים, וּזְקֵנִים לִנְבִיאִים,
> וּנְבִיאִים מְסָרוּהָ לְאַנְשֵׁי כְּנֶסֶת הַגְּדוֹלָה.
>
> *1 Moses received Torah from God at Sinai.*
> He transmitted it to Joshua,
> Joshua to the Elders, the Elders to the Prophets,
> the Prophets to the members of the Great Assembly.
>
> (Pirke Avot 1:1)

.... and now to us...

△ write one thing that's been transmitted to you from a previous generation

△ write one thing that you can pass on

194 Jewish Family Retreats

> אֵיזֶהוּ חָכָם?
> הַלּוֹמֵד מִכָּל אָדָם.
>
> **"Who is wise? The person who is open to learning from everyone.**
> (Pirke Avot 4:1)

△ Write down one thing that you've learned from your children/students.

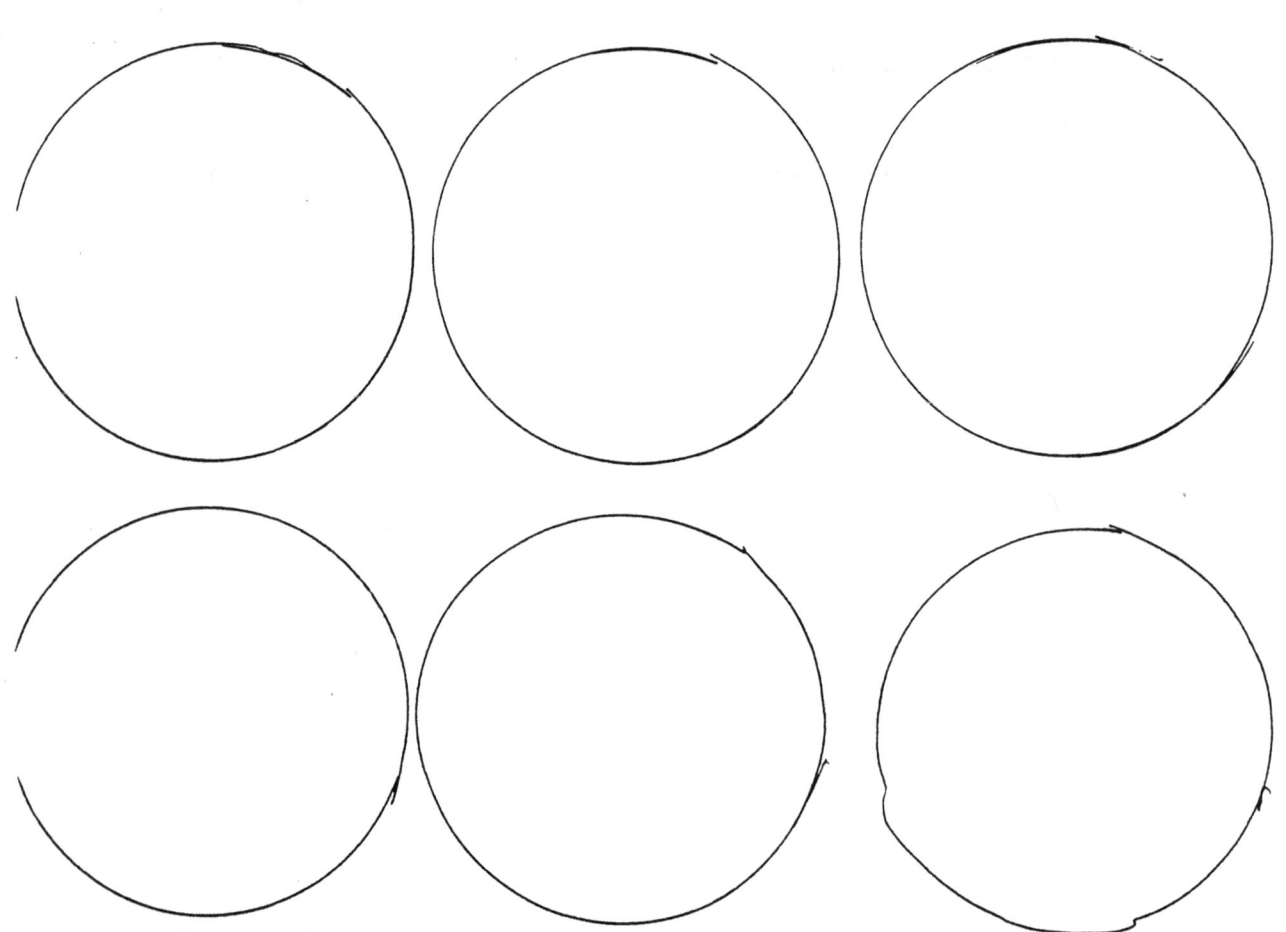

THE FAMILY CAMP SONG

here's the chorus:
> Family Camp is my camp.
> Family Camp is your camp.
> We work together —
> despite the weather!
> We sing and learn some
> And always have fun
> Family camp's the place for you and me!*

here's your family's verse:

_____

_____

_____

_____

_____

_____

Family camp's the place for you and me!

*Melody = "This Land Is Your Land"

It's been a Family Camp tradition to sum up our Family Camp experience in song during our closing celebration. Hers's the chorus of this years song. Your job, should you choose to accept it, is to write a verse with your family to sing together Sunday morning.

Sing to the tune of

♪♩ She'll Be Coming Round The Mountain

CHORUS

I went to Ramah Camp with my family

We knew it was the greatest place to be

We all learned, we all had fun

And made friends with everyone

Oh, Family Camp's the place for you and me!

_____

_____

_____

_____

* Any questions about this wonderful tradition? Ask these families- Felix, Brosbe, Toschi, or Gamson.

Birka HaMazon

★★★★★★★★★★★★★★★★★

Leader:
Friends, let us praise God.

Group:
The name of the Eternal be praised from now to eternity.

Leader:
Let us praise God of whose bounty we have partaken.

Group:
Let us praise our God of whose bounty we have partaken and by whose goodness we live.

Leader:
Ra-bo-tai, ne-va-reich!

Group:
Ye-hi sheim A-do-nai me-vo-rach
mei-a-ta ve-ad o-lam.

Leader:
Ye-hi sheim A-do-nai me-vo-rach
mei-a-ta
ve-ad olam.
Bi-re-shut ma-ra-nan ve-ra-ba-nan
ve-ra-bo-tai
ne-va-reich (E-lo-hei-nu)*
she-a-chal-nu mi-she-lo

Group:
Ba-ruch (E-lo-hei-nu) she-a-chal-nu
mi-she-lo
u-ve-tu-vo cha-yi-nu.

Leader:
Ba-ruch (E-lo-hei-nu) she-a-chal-nu
mi-she-lo
u-ve-tu-vo cha-yi-nu.
Baruch Hu u-va-ruch Shemo

Together:
Ba-ruch a-ta, A-do-nai, E-lo-hei-nu,
me-lech
ha-o-lam, ha-zan et ha-o-lam
ku-lo be-tu-vo be-chein, be-che-sed,
u-ve-ra-cha-mim
Hu-no-tein le-chem
le-chol ba-sar, ki le-o-lam chas-do.
U-ve-tu-vo

p. 1

---

ha-ga-dol, ki hu Eil zan u-me-far-neis
la-kol, u-mei-tiv
la-kol, u-mei-chin ma-zon
le-chol be-ri-yo-tav a-sher ba-ra.
Ba-ruch a-ta, A-do-nai, ha-zan
et ha-kol.

Through God's kindness, mercy and compassion all existence is eternally sustained. God is forever faithful. God's surpassing goodness fills all time and space. Sustenance there is for all. None need ever lack, no being ever want for food. We praise our God, the One, sustaining all.

Group:
Ka-ka-tuv, ve-a-chal-ta, ve-sa-va-ta,
u-vei-rach-ta et Adonai
E-lo-hei-cha, al ha-aretz
ha-tova asher na-tan lach.
Ba-ruch A-ta A-do-nai,
Al-ha-a-rets ve-al ha-mazon.

As it is written in Scripture: "You shall eat, be satisfied and praise Adonai your God for the good land given unto you. We praise you, O God, for the earth and for sustenance."

U-ve-nei Ye-ru-sha-la-yim ir
ha-ko-desh bi-me-hei-ra
be-ya-nei-nu.
Ba-ruch a-ta, A-do-nai,
bo-neh be-ra-cha-mav
Ye-ru-sha-la-yim. A-mein.

And build Jerusalem O God, speedily in our days.
We praise our God whose compassion ever builds Jerusalem.

On Shabbat:
Ha-ra-cha-man, hu yan-chi-lei-nu
yom she-ku-lo sha-bat u-me-nu-cha
le-cha-yei ha-o-la-mim.

All Merciful, may we inherit a Sabbath of eternal peace.

Leader:
O seh sha-lom bi-me-ro-mav,
hu ya-a-seh
sha-lom a-lei-nu, ve-al kol
Yis-ra-eil, ve-i-me-ru: A-mein.

p. 2

KABBALAT SHABBAT

Mah Yafeh
Mah Yafeh hayom shabbat Shalom
Mah yafeh hayom
Shabbat shalom

L'cha dodi (262)
L'cha dodi likrat kallah
p'nei shabbat n'kabbalah
Shamor v'zachor b'dibur echad
Hishmeanu el hamyuchad
Adonai echad ush'mo Echad
l'shem ul'tiferet v'lit'hela
Lcha dodi...

Mizmor Shir (266)
Tov l'hodot Lhodot ladonai
ul'zamer lshimcha elyon
L'hagid baboker baboker chazdecha
v'emunatcha balelot

V'shamru (294)
V'shamru v'nei yisrael Et hashabbat
Laasot et hashabat l'dorotam brit olam
Beini uvein b'nei yisrael ot he l'olam
ki sheshet yamin asa adonai et hashamayim v'et haretz
u'vayom hash'viee shavat va'yinafash

Shir Hamalot
Shir Hamalot b'shuv adonai
et shivat tzion
Hayinu k'cholmim
Shabbat Shalom u'mevorach

Shalom Rav (p. 302)

Shalom Rav al Yisrael amcha
Tasim l'olam;
Ki Ata hu melech adon l'chol ha'shalom
v'tov b'cynecha l'varech et amcha Yisrael
b'chol eyt u'v'chol sha'ah
b'shlomecha

Yedid Nefesh (p. 252)

Yedid nefesh, Av haRahaman,
M'shoch Avdecha el R'tzonecha
Yarutz avdecha, k'mo ayal,
Yishtahaveh el mul hadarecha
Ye'erav lo yedidotecha
m'nofet tzuf v'kol ta'am
Ya la la la la la ....

Memo

to: the counselors
from: Vicky and Janet
about: odds and ends
        (in no particular order)

1. Cherie will be handling the kitchen with assistance from Dawn, Annette, Brad, Varda, Annette and Jody if/when they're available. We hope that this will go pretty smoothly. Prior to most meals you will be with your campers so you will not be available to help but please make it a habit to check in with Cherie before meals and see if she needs any help with set up....and lend a hand after meals with the clean-up...most of which will involve getting the food cleared and put away and the tables wiped down.

    Etan and Elaine will take turns taking 3 or 4 of their campers to help set-up for lunch.

2. The supplies and games and sports equipment are all stored in Vicky's room, 11b. There are balls of various sizes and shapes, frisbees and aerobie and a 'shmerltz' along with badmitten raquests and birdies, some ping-pong balls and a kind of pitching horseshoes game. The craft supplies, the supplies for bubbles, most of the baking supplies and some of the game and idea books are also there. There are also some board games such as body-boggle, scan, othello, etc., Whatever you use -- **be sure to return it** when you return to the diningroom with your kids at the end of the activity. **This system for supplies and equipment will only work if you return stuff when you're finished so they other groups can use it.**

3. During group time -- Janet will be coming around to check that all is well and will be available if there is a problem.

4. Families will be eating meals together. At lunch and supper, as the kids finish eating and begin to get up and roam around, two of you should assign yourselves to sit and read to them or play quiet games, while the adults finish their meals and conversations. (Our 'veteran' counselors tell us that going two by two in alphbetical order works for this system.) We will call everyone back to the tables for Birkat HaMazon. We've asked the parents not to give kids permission to leave the diningroom.

5. For shmira -- we have given the parents some post-its to hang on their doors when they have checked in for the night. (Make sure they're all removed from the previous night when you begin the evening.) We have asked them **to check in with you if they come back before shmira is over and also use the tag**. We will give you a list with who's in which room and some stickers to use as a check-off system.

   The shmira set up for the cabins will be outside. The shmirah set up for the lodge can be in the hall. Organize yourselves as you like, but keep in mind that the first two nights it's important for there to be one counselor from each group at each spot.

   Remember to check at each door at <u>frequent regular</u> intervals.

6. We need your strong voices and 'modeling' at all events: singing, dovening dancing, birkat ha mazon, etc.

For example: at the Oneg Shabbat on Friday night we will need **extra help** with the dancing -- If you can **space yourselves out so you're evenly distributed** among our parents and kids you can facilitate everyone joining in without a break in the flow for instructions, etc., For "Tayish" help people get into couples and join in the dance yourself making couples with the kids.

7. Family Evening programs: join in, sit among families, help out where you see a problem or potential problem.

Family Fun night: This a traditional Shabbat Camp Saturday night activity. It consists of a round-robin of games at various sessions. Teams visit each station, rotating at the sound of the whistle or gong.

Vicky will be in charge of setting up and will give you your supplies, your station identification number and anything else you need. We'll try to set it up so that the groups move in a large circle around the area.

We will have 5 teams and 6 stations (meaning at each round one station will be empty.)

Since this is taking place <u>before</u> Havdallah, it will <u>still be Shabbat</u> and so we've invented a Shabbat score keeping system which uses stickers (reinforcements and stars). Each team will have its own score sheet with its name on top and a number corresponding to each station which they will carry with them as they rotate. Keep track of the points (in your head or as you go; this will vary with whether your activity leaves your hands free or not). Use star stickers for five points and reinforcements for ones.

assignments: #1: zig-zag walk (or for those over 6: zig-zag hop): Lewis
    #2: blockhead: Elana
    #3: the dress-up relay: Lisa
    #4: memory board: Etan
    #5: feather relay: David
    #6: gum and gloves pass: Elaine
Andrea, Jody, Annette: float and help out

Don't worry about the details here. We will have time later in the week to prepare for this.

8. Janet and her family, and Vicky will be living in 11A and 11B

9. **WE WILL HAVE A BRIEF STAFF MEETING EVERYDAY AFTER LUNCH (at the beginning of rest).**

10. **HAVE FUN!!!!!**

counselor resources:

suggested games for <u>our older</u> group: All of these are good games for Shabbat

a note on leading and teaching games: be sure your staff all know the game. It helps to practice it first. When introducing a new game, demonstrate it first...and then a counselor should be 'it' first or be the one to go first.

If you need any supplies (sports stuff, deck of cards, bandana, etc., see Janet or Vicky at the event predeecing group time.

indoor: small group: **cards** (play go-fish or memory or build card houses)
 board games such as Sorry and Scan
 hand games such as rock, scissors paper (even, niyyar, misparayim)
 whole group: **charades** -- divide kids into groups, whisper a topic to each group and give them 3 or so minutes to prep; for ex: round one: give each a machine; round two: give each a Bible story; round three: give each a Jewish holiday, a TV show; etc., We've also brought a set of alef-bet cards -- kids can pick a card at random and take one minute to form that letter using all team members in a body sculpture

 circle games such as: <u>concentration</u>, <u>the Rabbi's Cat</u>, <u>A my Name is .....</u>, <u>Hot Potato</u>, <u>Indian Chief</u>; <u>pass the squeeze</u> (send one, send one in each direction, make it fancy with double and triple squeezes; add the sound "ooh" to go with the squeeze; then add "ah" and send it the other way, etc.,) <u>Face Pass</u> -- make a strange, distorted or funny face; turn to a person on one side of you; that person has to copy your face as if he or she were your mirror; both of you face the group so all can see how much alike you look; then, your mirror makes a new face and passes it on around to the person on the other side of her, and so on around the circle; <u>Ha-ha</u>; <u>knots</u>: stand in a circle shoulder to shoulder and place all hands in the center; everyone take 2 other hands (don't hold both hands of the same person and don't hold hands with the person on either side of you): Untangle yourselves without letting go of any hands; <u>Stand-up</u>: Sit on the ground back-to-back with your partner, knees bent and elbows linked. Stand up together. When the first pair has this mastered, add a third person. Keep adding until the whole group does a stand-up; **name games**: <u>Dr. Memory</u>: (Introduce self "I'm Joe." Next person introduces herself plus you: "Hi! I'm Sarah. This is Joe." Keep it going till you've gone around the circle.) <u>Name Echo</u>: Say your name with a sound effect -- after you say yours everyone echoes it. Then the next person says his/her name with a sound and the group echoes him/her. (Examples: Josh, said like a choo-choo train: Josh josh josh josh--woo-woo! OR Michael said like a kitten meowing.) <u>Name</u>

Ripple: Start with someone else's name. Say it...everyone repeats it going around the circle till it reaches that person; that person then chooses someone else's name and starts it rippling around the circle. Make this more complex by choosing a name and a motion (Rebecca with a deep knee bend). The name and the motion goes in a chosen direction around the circle like a wave until it reaches the person whose name is Rebecca. She doesn't repeat her name, she immediately says someone the name of someone else in the circle and adds a motion (Coby with a jumping jack).

good games to end a session with: _Spirals:_ Stand in a circle holding hands. The leader releases the hand of one neighbor and begins, pulling the human rope behind her, to walk around the outside of the circle. The other person who broke hands remains stationary. The human rope circles around and around the stationery person into a tighter and tighter coil until all the players are wrapped around each other. (The best way to unfold is from the center. Still holding hands, the person in the middle ducks down and begins to crawl out throught the forest of legs. The whole group follows down and through, uncoiling until you're a circle again; and don't forget to do a _Group Lap-sit_

outside/active games: all the usual sports; _ga-ga_; _frisbee_ ; all kinds of _tag_, _mother-may-I?_ _Redlight/Green light_, _steal the bagel_; _amoeba_ also called _blob_ -- the amoeba starts chasing people --the first person tagged joins hands and becomes part of the amoeba; they link arms and continue ...the next person tagged also links arms and so on until everyone has become part of the amoeba or the blob; (2 variations to note: amoeba is often played in slow-motion so it _could_ be played indoors ; also in amoeba sometimes the amoebas split into two 2's when they become 4;) _catch the dragon's tail_--Everyone lines up putting their arms around the waist of the person infront; The last person tucks and bandana in the back of his belt as a tail; At the signal, the dragon's head begins to chase its tail, the object being to try to snatch the bandana. When the head captures the tail, everyone turns around, the head tucks in the bandana and becomes the new tail and the second to the head becomes the new head. With lots of flat safe space and energy you can play two dragons each trying to catch the other's tail; _schmerltz_ --this is catch with a new gadget -- a schmerltz is a long sock with a ball knotted in; the thrower twirls it around underhanded a few times and lets it fly to a partner or team; it is caught in the air by the tail only;

These are _suggestions_ -- be creative and have fun!!!!!

IF:

don't forget there is nerf sports stuff

SHABBAT activities for Younger Children

11:00 A.M. - NOON
4:00 P.M. - 5:45 P.M. (you'll have snack to take along)

Inside--playdough
        bristle blocks
        lincoln logs
        board games
        flannel boards
        stories/books
        puppets
        sticker pictures
        playdough sculptures
        nerf sports stuff

Outside--playground - and hike around camp
        walk to feed horses and ducks
        parachute
        ball games
        circle games
        scavenger hunts around the camp

SUNDAY activities for Young Children

have kids prepare something for their mothers- ideas are:
making special tablecloths, [placemats for mom
make necklaces
write mom stories- dictated to counselors
do a short skit or vignette
sing mom a song
prepare part of the lunch
make mothers' day cakes
make potpourri
pressed flowers
wind chimes

 or

THE Family Camp er

Why Evaluation?

Sunday morning's program includes a very important session for adults, devoted to the evaluation of Family Camp. We urge everyone to please attend that session to help us think about Family Camp for future years.

Family Camp has been a two year joint project of Camp Ramah in California and the Melton Research Center of The Jewish Theological Seminary. Melton is a Jewish education research and development center, a kind of educational think tank, which for many years has been involved in curriculum planning, teacher education, and educational development. Both Vicky Kelman and Ruth Zielenziger are Melton staff members. Family Camp emerged out of Vicky's work at Melton developing a series of materials for parents and children entitled Together. The Together publications led to workshops for parents and kids and eventually became the idea for Family Camp. Vicky's work with Glenn and Camp Ramah in California allowed that idea to become a reality.

Camp Ramah and the Melton Center are both committed to the concept of camping as an educational opportunity and to the family as the key religious educator in a child's life. It is this educational orientation that has distinguished the Ramah movement throughout its forty year history.

Of course, evaluation is at the heart of any good educational venture: it allows us the chance to think and talk about what we've done and to make changes and adjustments for the future.

PLEASE help us in this important project by joining in the evaluation session on Sunday morning.

Todah Rabbah!
(Thanks a lot!)

September 4, 1988
22 Elul 5748

RAMAH FAMILY CAMP II

EVALUATION

The best way for a staff to learn about a program it has run is to ask participants for their honest evaluation. These evaluations are <u>anonymous</u>. Please answer the questions from your own individual perspective.

I. Family Camp has many different aspects to it. Please note from 1 to 5 your satisfaction with each of these aspects. 5 represents highly satisfied. 1 represents "not at all satisfied".

1. Communications <u>prior</u> to camp   1 2 3 4 5
2. Orientation to camp <u>on first afternoon</u>   1 2 3 4 5
3. Communication of information <u>during</u> camp   1 2 3 4 5
4. Housing (what kind of housing were you in? _____)   1 2 3 4 5
5. Meals   1 2 3 4 5
6. Recreational facilities   1 2 3 4 5
7. T'fillah (prayer services)   1 2 3 4 5
8. Programming for Yedidim (2-5)   1 2 3 4 5
9. Programming for Keshet (6,7,8)   1 2 3 4 5
10. Programming for Shemesh (9,10,11)   1 2 3 4 5
11. Programming for Chaverim (12,13,14)   1 2 3 4 5
12. Classes for the children   1 2 3 4 5
13. Quality of the counselors   1 2 3 4 5
14. Classes for adults   1 2 3 4 5
15. Adult evening programs   1 2 3 4 5
16. Family programs   1 2 3 4 5
17. Quality of the teachers (for both adults and children)   1 2 3 4 5
18. Quality of the administrative staff   1 2 3 4 5
19. The total 5 day Family Camp experience   1 2 3 4 5

II.

1. How did you hear about Family Camp?

2. Why did it interest you?

3. If there were areas which were particularly outstanding, please list them.

4. If you rated any of the areas on the previous page as less than satisfactory, please give us some suggestions for how they can be improved.

5. Did you have any expectations of Family Camp which were not met by the program?

6. Please comment on the balance that was struck between time to be together with your family and time to be on your own?

7. How would you rate Family Camp in terms of the opportunity to meet new people and make new friends?

8. Do you feel that a sense of community was established among the families here? Would you have wanted more or less sense of community?

9. Planning and leading tefillot (prayer services) for a group disparate as ours in background, age and attention span is one of the more complex undertakings of Family Camp. How did they work for you and your family?

10. How would you evaluate the opportunity for Jewish learning?

11. What are you and your family taking home from Camp?

12. (a) Thinking ahead, what form(s) of follow-up, if any, would you like to see in the coming year?

   More specifically, would you be interested in:

   (b) Having a Sunday afternoon reunion?   yes   no   unsure

   (c) Having a reunion weekend at Camp?   yes   no   unsure

   (d) Receiving mailings at home about
       Jewish celebrations?   yes   no   unsure

   (e) Having Shabbat dinners with other
       families?   yes   no   unsure

   (f) Attending Family Camp again next summer?   yes   no   unsure

13. Please add any other comments, suggestions and reflections.

III. If you attended last summer's Family Camp, please answer these questions, too:

1. Why did you come back to Family Camp?

2. What kind of impact, if any, do you think last summer's Family Camp had on your family? Be as specific as you can.

3. Does it seem to you that the impact of this summer's experience will be different? If so, how? If not, why not?

4. Comment on the differences between last year's Family Camp and this year's:

5. Did you feel that the increased size of the group made a difference? (If so, how?)

6. Do you think you would come if Family Camp were longer?

Shabbat Camp
Evaluation
14 May 1989

1 Please rank each of the following areas from 1(low) to 10 high):
   Add a short comment if you wish:

1. accomodations: _____

2. meals: _____

3. kids' program with counselors:_____

4. family programs: _____

5. study for adults:_____

6. tefilla (services): _____

7. site: _____

8. music: _____

9. staff:_____

10. the whole weekend _____

11 Please comment briefly on how you found the balance
between structured time and free time:

12. What were the best parts of the program for your family?

13 What changes would you suggest we make for the next Shabbat Camp?

14. What kind of followup (if any) would you like? mailings? an adult get-together? a family Shabbat dinner? a family outing? etc.,

15. Choose three adjectives that describe your family's experience here at Shabbat camp this weekend:

17. Would you like to come back? Why?/ Why not?

18. Anything else you want to say:

Your evaluations will help us to improve our program so we can continue to provide effectively for the Jewish educational needs of our community.

Evaluation questions
Five Day Shabbat Camp
June 1990

(dictated at a 10-15 minute session; people wrote answers on yellow legal paper; names optional;)

1. How did you hear about this program?

2. (Y/N) Would you like to do this again?

3. (Y/N) Would you be willing to network to other families? (i.e., if we sent you a dozen flyers would you be willing to give them to families you know/think would be interested in this kind of experience or would benefit from it?)

4. In one sentence: What was your favorite moment here? (a one sentence snapshot;)

5. In one sentence: What do you think will be your family's next step Jewishly? (i.e., what do you think you'll do that you havn't been doing until now?)

6. In a paragraph: What an short note to a friend describing the experience your family had here.

7. Anything else you want to add....

Ramah Family Camp
Evaluation questions;
August 90 and 91

questions posted on wall;
people wrote answers on lined paper;
20 -25 minutes;

1. If this is your first time: how did you hear about us?

2. What did you come for? What brought you here?

3. Describe a **family** highlight from the week

4. Describe a **personal** highlight from the week

5. What do you think is your family's next Jewish step?

6. What do you think we should add to the program?

7. What should we subtract (to make room for what you want to add)?

8. anything else you want to tell me

9. **T/F**   We are coming back if we can.

10. Choose 3 words which describe you family's experience this week.

AND --- give the whole experience a score from 1 (low) to 10 (high)

12 Bibliography and Resource List

Family Education

Jewish Materials for Direct Family Programming

Alper, Janice, ed. *Learning Together: A Sourcebook on Jewish Family Education.* Denver: Alternatives in Religious Education, 1987. (3945 South Oneida, Denver, CO 80237; 800/346-7779) A potpourri of tried and tested family programs from different settings; contains a fantastic bibliography.

Building Jewish Life Series. Los Angeles: Torah Aura Productions, 1989. (4423 Fruitvale Avenue, Los Angeles, CA 90058; 213/585-7312) A series of books and activity books for grades K through two; designed to be used in school and with parents at home.

Kelman, Vicky. *Together: A Child-Parent Kit.* New York: Melton Research Center, Jewish Theological Seminary, 1983-84. (3080 Broadway, New York, N.Y. 10027; 212/678-8031) A series of nine interactive kits for ages eight through ten and parents to enjoy, learn from and have a good time with at home; set includes a User's Guide for the educator interested in implementing the *Together* program.

———. *Windows.* New York: Melton Research Center, Jewish Theological Seminary, 1990. A series of four family programs for sixth and seventh graders and their parents, designed to cover some of the important pre-Bar/Bat Mitzvah topics (God, ethics and law, Bar/Bat Mitzvah and community/synagogue).

Wolfson, Ron. *The Art of Jewish Living* Series. Los Angeles: Federation of Jewish Men's Clubs and University of Judaism in Los Angeles, 1985-90. (15600 Mulholland Drive, Los Angeles, CA 90077; 310/476-9777) Shabbat, Passover and Hanukkah are available in this series, each with coordinated audiotapes. These are written for adults as guides to creating and guiding family celebrations and contain everything from interviews with "real" families to background information to recipes.

Theology, Faith Development and Religious Perspectives on the Family

Introduction to Jewish Theology

Gillman, Neil. *Sacred Fragments: Recovering Theology for the Modern Jew.* Philadelphia: Jewish Publication Society, 1990.

Kushner, Harold. *When Bad Things Happen to Good People.* New York: Schocken Books, 1981.

Wolpe, David. *The Healer of Shattered Hearts: A Jewish View of God.* New York: Henry Holt and Co., 1990.

Other

Chesto, Kathleen. *Family Centered Intergenerational Religious Education (FIRE).* Kansas City: Sheed and Ward, 1988. (115 E. Armour Blvd., P.O. Box 419492, Kansas City, MO 64141; 800/333-7373) A five-year havurah-type curriculum focusing on the spiritual and prayer life of the family; a "must read."

Coles, Robert. *The Spiritual Life of Children.* Boston: Houghton Mifflin, 1990. What kind of "theology" are our children thinking about?

Fitzpatrick, Jean Grasso. *Something More: Nurturing Your Child's Spiritual Growth.* New York: Viking, 1991. A thoughtful and useful resource.

Gellman, Marc, and Thomas Hartman. *Where Does God Live? Questions and Answers for Parents and Children.* New York: Triumph Books, 1991. Cowritten by a rabbi and a Roman Catholic monsignor; provocative.

Parks, Sharon. *The Critical Years: Young Adults and the Search for Meaning, Faith and Commitment.* San Francisco: HarperCollins, 1991. Understanding the search for meaning during the young adult (postadolescent but preadult) phase of life.

Religious Education 83, no. 4 (Fall 1988). An entire issue devoted to spiritual life of the family.

Sawin, Margaret. *Family Enrichment with Family Clusters.* Valley Forge, Pa.: Judson Press, 1979. A classic in religious family education; written from a family-systems viewpoint.

Stokes, Kenneth. *Faith Is a Verb.* Mystic, Conn.: Twenty-third Publications, 1989. A good introduction to faith development.

Westerhoff, John. *Will Our Children Have Faith?* San Francisco: Harper and Row, 1976.

Important General Literature on the Family

Blankenhorn, David, Steven Bayme, and Jean Elshtain, eds. *Rebuilding the Nest.* Milwaukee: Family Service America, 1990.

Napier, Gus, and Carl Whitaker. *The Family Crucible.* San Francisco: Harper and Row, 1978.

Nichols, Michael. *The Power of the Family.* New York: Simon and Schuster, 1988.

Olson, David, Hamilton McCubbin, Howard Barnes, Andrew Larsen, Marla Muxen, and Marc Wilson. *Families: What Makes Them Work.* Newbury Park, Calif.: Sage Publications, 1989.

Satir, Virginia. *Peoplemaking.* Palo Alto, Calif.: Science and Behavior Books, 1972. A classic; an ideal introduction to family systems.

Stinnet, Nick, and John DeFrain. *Secrets of Strong Families.* Boston: Little, Brown and Co., 1985.

Wallerstein, Judith, and Sandra Blakeslee. *Second Chances.* New York: Ticknor and Fields, 1989. Family members a decade after divorce.

Programmatic Resources

Jewish Resources

Beiner, Stan. *Sedra Scenes.* Denver: Alternatives in Religious Education, 1982. Skits for each Torah portion; grades six and up.

Cone, Mollie. *The Shma Storybooks.* New York: Union of American Hebrew Congregations, 1973. A series of three books of good teaching stories.

Goldberg, Sorel, and Barbara Kadden. *Teaching Torah.* Denver: Alternatives in Religious Education, 1984. Lots of activities coordinated with each Torah portion.

Grishaver, Joel. *Being Torah.* Los Angeles: Torah Aura Productions, 1987. Torah text for fourth through sixth grades.

———. *Bible People.* 3 vols. Denver, Alternatives in Religious Education, 1980–82. Bible stories.

Harlow, Jules, ed. *Lessons from Our Living Past.* New York: Behrman House Publishers, 1972. Good source of stories and legends.

———. *Stories from Our Living Past.* New York: Behrman House Publishers, 1974.

Kushner, Lawrence. *The Book of Miracles.* New York: Union of American Hebrew Congregations, 1987. "Spiritual" stories for kids aged about nine and up.

Ray, Eric. *Sofer.* Los Angeles: Torah Aura Productions, 1986. *Sofer* is Hebrew for scribe. A close look at the writing of a Torah scroll; use in conjunction with a "Torah roll" or other similar Torah activities.

Stories

Cohen, Barbara. *The Carp in the Bathtub.* Rockville, Md.: Kar-Ben Copies, 1972. The classic "pet fish versus gefilte fish" story.

Fox, Mem. *Wilfred George McDonald Partridge.* La Jolla, Calif.: Kane-Miller Book Publishers, 1984. A small boy tries to discover the meaning of "memory" so he can restore that of an elderly friend.

Mills, Lauren. *The Rag Coat.* Boston: Little, Brown and Co., 1991. Minna proudly wears her new coat of clothing scraps to school, where other children laugh at its strangeness until she tells them the stories behind the scraps.

Palacco, Patricia. *The Keeping Quilt.* New York: Simon and Schuster, 1988. A homemade quilt ties together the lives of four generations of an immigrant Jewish family.

Games

Flugelman, Andrew, ed. *The New Games Book.* Garden City, N.Y.: Doubleday and Co., 1976.

Le Fevre, Dale. *New Games for the Whole Family.* New York: Putnam Publishing Group, 1988.

Maguire, Jack. *Hopscotch, Hangman, Hot Potato and HaHaHa.* New York: Prentice Hall Press, 1990.

Orlick, Terry. *The Second Cooperative Sports and Games Book.* New York: Pantheon Books, 1982.

Weinstein, Matt, and Joel Goodman. *Playfair*. San Luis Obispo, Calif.: Impact Publishers, 1980.

Outdoors/Nature

General

Cornell, Joseph. *Listening to Nature*. Nevada City, Calif.: Dawn Publications, 1987. (14618 Tyler Foote Road, Nevada City, CA 95959; 916/292-3484) This book and the following one are the classics in this area; discrete easily replicable experiences.

———. *Sharing the Joy of Nature*. Nevada City, Calif.: Dawn Publications, 1989.

Milord, Susan. *The Kids' Nature Book*. Carlotte, Vt.: Williamson Publishing, 1989. Lots of ideas.

Rockwell, Robert. *Hug a Tree*. Mt. Rainier, Md.: Gryphon House, 1986. Lots of ideas for preschoolers.

Shaffer, Carolyn, and Erica Fielder. *City Safaris*. San Francisco: Sierra Club Books, 1987.

Sisson, Edith. *Nature with Children of All Ages*. Englewood Cliffs, N.J.: Prentice-Hall, 1982. Lots of ideas.

Astronomy

Jobb, Jamie. *The Night Sky Book*. Boston: Little, Brown and Co., 1977.

Rey, N. A. *Find the Constellations*. Boston: Houghton Mifflin Co., 1976.

Stories

Cooney, Barbara. *Miss Rumphius*. New York: Penguin, Puffin Books, 1982.

Suess, Dr. *The Lorax*. New York: Random House, 1971.

Van Allsburg, Chris. *Just a Dream*. Boston: Houghton Mifflin Co., 1990.

Crafts

Ayture-Scheele, Zulal. *The Great Origami Book.* New York: Sterling Publishing, 1987.

Blocksma, Mary, and Dewey Blocksma. *Space Crafting.* New York: Prentice-Hall, 1986. Things to make and fly.

Botermans, Jack, and Alice Weve. *Kite Flight.* New York: Henry Holt and Co., 1986.

Greger, Margaret. *Kites for Everyone.* Richland, Wash.: Greger, 1984. (1425 Marshall, Richland, WA) Clear directions, diagrams and patterns; advice for different age groups.

McGraw, Sheila. *Papier-Mache for Kids.* Willowdale, Ontario: Firefly Books, 1991. Great ideas for newspaper and paste.

Morris, Cambell. *Best Paper Aircraft.* New York: Putnam Publishing Group, 1986. A zillion models; fun with 8½" × 11" paper.

———. *More Best Paper Aircraft.* New York: Putnam Publishing Group, 1988.

Smithsonian. *Science Activity Book.* Smithsonian Family Learning Project. New York: GMG Publishing, Galison Books, 1987.

Temko, Florence. *Jewish Origami.* Union City, Calif.: Heian International, 1991.

Walter, Virginia. *Great Newspaper Crafts.* New York: Sterling Publishing, 1991. Great ideas for newspaper and paste.

Music

Jewish Music Audiotapes

Beged Kefet. *Lifeline.* (Dist. by Leon Sher, 78 Glendale Ave., Livingston, NJ 07039)

Cotler, Doug. *Listen.* (Dist. by A Major Studio, 14746 Archwood St., Van Nuys, CA 91405; 818/908-1440)

Friedman, Debbie. *And the Youth Shall See Visions* (1981).[1]
———. *And You Shall Be a Blessing* (1989).[2]
———. *Ani Ma'amin* (1976).

---

[1] Includes "Oseh Shalom" and "And You Shall Love the Lord Your God."

[2] "L'chi Lach"

———. *Debbie Friedman Live at the Del* (1990).[3]
———. *Miracles and Wonders* (1992).
———. *Not by Might—Not by Power* (1974).[4]
———. *Sing unto God* (1972).
(All dist. by Sounds Write Productions, Inc., P.O. Box 608078, San Diego, CA 92119)

Kol B'Seder. *The Bridge.*[5]
———. *Shalom Rav.*[6]
———. *Sparks of Torah.*
(All dist. by Kol B'Seder, 1224 Dempster, Evanston, IL 60202)

Kol Haneshamah: Songs, Blessings and Rituals for the Home.[7] Wyncote, Pa.: Federation of Reconstructionist Congregations and Havurot. (Church Road and Greenwood Avenue, Suite 300, Wyncote, PA 19095) Includes Kiddush, two versions of Birkat haMazon, traditional Shabbat songs, a few Hanukkah songs and some Israeli standards; coordinated with Blessings booklet (chapter 7, footnote. 5).

Taubman, Craig. *Beginnings.*[8]
———. *We Were as Dreamers.*[9]
———. *Yad B'Yad.*[10]
(All dist. by Los Angeles Hebrew High School, 15339 Saticoy St., Van Nuys, CA 91406)
———. *Master of All Things.*
———. *Encore.*
(Both dist. by Sweet Louise Productions, 13226 Otsego St., Sherman Oaks, CA 91423)

Jewish Music Songbooks

Friedman, Debbie. *Blessings.* San Diego, Calif.: Sounds Write Productions, 1990.

———. *Miracles and Wonders.* San Diego, Calif.: Sounds Write Productions, 1992.

---

[3]"The Alef-Bet Song," "On Wings of Eagles" and "V'Ha'er Einenu"

[4]"Etz Hayim"

[5]"Ani V'Ata"

[6]"Shalom Rav"

[7]"Mah Yafeh HaYom"

[8]"V'Shinantam"

[9]"Va'Anachnu" and "HaTov"

[10]"Yad B'Yad"

NIFTY's 50! Songbook. New York: Transcontinental Music Publications. (838 Fifth Ave., New York, NY 10021)

Taubman, Craig. *Songbook.* Sherman Oaks, Calif.: Sweet Louise Productions.

Other Songs Mentioned in Book

"The Family Song." In *To See the World through Jewish Eyes* (album). New York: Union of American Hebrew Congregations. This is a fun song for families to learn and sing, but it does imply that everyone has an Ima (mommy) and an Aba (daddy). The staff for the retreat can listen to the song and decide whether or not to include it, or how to adapt the words to be more inclusive for your population.

"Hinay Tov Me'od." In *NIFTY's 50!*

"Make Those Waters Part." In Doug Mishkin, *Woody's Children* (audiotape). Washington, D.C.: Midoaks Records, 1987. (1801 K Street N.W., Suite 1100K, Washington, DC 20006) Also found in *NIFTY's 50!*

"Shavua Tov, May You Have a Good Week." (Also called "Havdalah.") In *Especially Jewish Symbols* (audiotape). Denver, Colo.: Alternatives in Religious Education, 1977. Also found in *NIFTY's 50!*

Other Audiotapes

Banana Slug String Band. *Songs for the Earth.* (Dist. by Exploring New Horizons, 555 Benjamin Holt Dr., Stockton, CA 95207) This tape and the next contain great nature/outdoor/ecology songs.

———. *Dirt Made my Lunch.* (Dist. by Music for Little People, P.O. Box 1460, Redway, CA 95560)

Thomas, Marlo, and friends. *Free to Be . . . a Family.* Hollywood, Calif.: A & M Records. (P.O. Box 118, Hollywood, CA 90078) Songs about the variety of families in which children live today; also available as a book of the same title (New York: Bantam Books, 1987).

13 Glossary

Alef-Bet: The alphabet

Aliyah: Going up to the Torah and reciting the blessings before and after one reading (pl., *aliyot*)

B'Hatzlaha: Good luck

Barukh Ha Shem: Thank God! (lit., may God be blessed)

Berakha: A blessing

Berakhot: Blessings

Birkat haMazon: The blessing recited after meals

Cherkassiya: A circle dance

Elul: The last month of the Jewish year

Erev Shabbat: Friday evening

Haftarah: A reading from the Prophets that complements the weekly Torah portion; read on Shabbat, holidays, the first day of each month and fast days

Haggadah: The book that contains the retelling of the exodus from Egypt and the ritual for the Passover seder

Halakhic: Pertaining to the framework of Jewish law

Hallah: The bread eaten at the beginning of Shabbat and holiday meals

HaMotzi: The blessing recited over bread, before meals

Hanukkah: The holiday celebrating the rededication of the Temple in the days of the Maccabees

Haroset: A mixture of fruit, nuts and wine, which is eaten as part of the Passover seder

Havdalah: The Saturday evening ceremonial closure to the Shabbat

Havurah: Fellowship group

Kabbalat Shabbat: The Friday evening service (lit., welcoming Shabbat)

Kasher: To make something kosher

Kashrut: Observance of the laws of keeping kosher

Kiddush: The blessing recited over wine at Shabbat and holiday meals; also, a light refreshment served after morning services on those days

Kippah: A skull cap; yarmulke (pl., *kippot*)

Matzah: Unleavened bread that replaces regular bread on Passover

Mayim: A circle dance

Mezuzot: Decorative containers placed on the door frame of a Jewish home, which hold parchment on which the first and second paragraphs of the Shma are written

Midrash: Classic Jewish literature that interprets Scripture (usually in the form of teaching stories)

Mishkan: The portable sanctuary that the Israelites constructed and traveled with in the desert

Mishpaha: Family

Musaf: The additional service added following Shaharit on Shabbat, holidays and the first day of a new month

Niggun: Song with few or no words

Oneg Shabbat: A Friday evening Shabbat celebration (lit., the joy of Shabbat)

Parashat haShavua: The weekly Torah portion (reading)

Purim: The holiday recounted in the Biblical book of Esther, in which Esther and her cousin Mordecai save the Jewish people from destruction

Rosh haShana: The New Year

Se'udah shlishit: The Saturday evening pre-Havdalah meal (lit., the third [Shabbat] meal)

Seder: The ritual dinner at which the exodus from Egypt is retold and reexperienced

Shabbat: The Sabbath, celebrated from sundown on Friday evening until the emergence of three stars on Saturday evening

Shaharit: The morning service

Shavua Tov: Have a good week! (The greeting for the end of Havdalah, which is the beginning of a new week)

Shavuot: The two-day holiday that celebrates the giving of the Torah

Shmirah: In the context of camp, the babysitting system (lit., guarding, taking care)

Shofar: The ram's horn blown daily during the month of Elul and featured prominently in the liturgy of the High Holy Days

Siddur: Prayerbook

Sofer: Scribe; a person trained to write Torah scrolls and the scrolls that go inside tefillin and mezuzot

Tallit: Prayer shawl

Talmud: The key work of rabbinic Judaism (c. 500 C.E.), which consists of a record of legal discussions

Tefilla: Prayer or prayer services

Tefillin: Phylacteries; small leather boxes containing biblical verses that are attached to one's arm and around one's head during the morning service

Teshuva: Return or turning (to the right path), usually meaning "repentance"

Tikkun olam: Working to make the world a better place (lit., fixing the world)

Tyish: A dance similar to the Virginia Reel

Tzedakah: Contribution of money (or other material things) for tikkun olam; from the Hebrew word for justice and often translated "charity"

Tzitzit: The specially tied tassels in the four corners of the tallit

U'N'Taneh Tokef: One of the central prayers of the High Holy Days liturgy

Yom Kippur: The Day of Atonement; a fast day; the holiest day of the Jewish calendar

Note on Transliteration

kh = khaf (כ)

h = het (ח)
(both can be pronounced like the *ch* in Bach)

tz = Tzadi (צ)
(pronounced like the *zz* in pizza)